THE
AUTHENTIC
WITNESS

"One way only will command respect and have power to persuade: and that is the Church's manner of being, the way she is, as she lives by the renewing power of Christ, for all to feel and see. I firmly believe that, without knowing it, this is what the world is waiting for."

—the closing lines from Hendrik Kraemer's
WHY CHRISTIANITY OF ALL RELIGIONS?

THE
AUTHENTIC
WITNESS

Credibility and Authority

by

C. Norman Kraus

WILLIAM B. EERDMANS PUBLISHING COMPANY
GRAND RAPIDS, MICHIGAN

Library of Congress Cataloging in Publication Data

Kraus, Clyde Norman.
  The authentic witness.

  1. Church. 2. Sociology, Christian.
I. Title.
BV600.2.K67   261.8   78-24012
ISBN 0-8028-1785-8

To Ruth
whose constant support
and shared insights
have made this project
possible

CONTENTS

Preface   9

Introduction: Authenticity, Discipleship, and
  Mission   13
   I. Incarnation, the Prototype of Authentic
      Witness   27
   II. Contextualizing the Witness—The Discerning
      Community   51
   III. Individual-in-Community—Biblical
      Perspectives   76
   IV. Individual and Community—Historical
      Developments   96
   V. Hallmarks of Authentic Community   118
   VI. The Church as a Sign in Protestant Theology   140
   VII. Authentic Community, a Sign of the
      Kingdom   155
   VIII. Community as Authentic Witness   172

Index   195

PREFACE

In THE EARLY 1960s COLIN WILLIAMS WROTE TWO
small books on the church entitled respectively *Where in the
World?* and *What in the World?* These titles represent quite
accurately the major concern of Protestant theology. Luther
located the visible church where the effects of the preached
Word were to be seen. Calvin and the Reformed tradition
were more concerned to redefine the nature and structure of
the church—the "what" in the world. Neither of these traditions at its source was vitally concerned with the question of
the visible church's mission in the world. That concern was
left to what is sometimes called the "radical Reformation" or
Anabaptism.

The question which was central for Anabaptism was
neither where nor what, but *how?* Jesus had characterized his
disciple church as *in* the world but not *of* the world. How is
the visible church in the world? What is its mission in God's
plan for history? How is it related to the coming kingdom?
What are its authenticating marks? It was only on the fringes
of Lutheranism in movements like that led by Thomas
Münzer that these questions were seriously reconsidered, but
they were at the heart of the Anabaptist movement.

Serious wrestling with these questions led the leaders at
Schleitheim (1527) and later Menno Simons to establish
separated but open communities of faithful disciples in the

9

world. It led the first generation Hutterites to organize their remarkable evangelistic missions to their fellow countrymen in Europe. It also led to Melchior Hofmann's quietism in the hope of an immediate return of Christ, as well as the violence of Münster where the church attempted to set up the kingdom by coercion. Our point here is not that correct answers were always found, but rather that the questions were raised afresh.

The question, "How in the world?" has come center stage again as the church in the twentieth century looks seriously at its mission in the world. In one world missionary conference after another, whether it be under the auspices of the "Ecumenical" or "Evangelical" forces, the questions are raised. What is the *role* of the church in world history? What *strategies* are appropriate to its mission? What is the relation of the church's *life* in authentic community and the *message* it proclaims? What are the identifying marks of *authenticity?* How can the message be *contextualized* without being compromised? Role and identity are major issues.

This essay poses authenticity rather than orthodoxy as the proper criterion for identifying the church, Christ's body, in the world. Traditionally the question has been discussed as the "marks of the *true* church." In Protestantism the criterion for genuineness has been orthodoxy. A correct theology preserved in creeds and in the preaching ministry of the church identifies and legitimates it as the church of Christ. When liberalism challenged the orthodoxy of seventeenth-century scholastic theology, it in effect merely substituted its own rational and empirical orthodoxies. Neither conservative nor liberal Protestantism has reckoned seriously with the criterion of authenticity in life and strategy as a crucial mark of churchly identification.

The essay further defines *authentic witness* as the key factor in identifying the body of Christ in the world, in contrast to correct organization or clerical structure, perfection in lifestyle, or ecstatic experience of Holy Spirit power. The hallmark of the Jesus movement in history is authentic relationship—the reconciliation of the human family in

Christ. The "true church" is the authentic community of witness.

This is a theological essay which I hope will catch the attention of the concerned layperson as well as the professional church and missionary community. Therefore, I have worked hard to avoid theological jargon, but it has not always been possible. Where traditional terms have become misleading because of popular usage, I have sometimes returned to original New Testament words, but in each case I have defined them so that my own meanings will be clear. In an undertaking of this kind it becomes obvious again how important it is to establish a community of discourse as a basis for communication!

C. Norman Kraus
Center for Discipleship
Goshen College, 1978

AUTHENTICITY, DISCIPLESHIP, AND MISSION

ONE DAY A STRAY CAT WANDERED INTO THE AREA where an Indian guru and his disciples sat on the ground meditating. The cat took a fancy to the guru and began rubbing himself against his back, purring all the while. After some time the guru became annoyed at the distraction, so taking a piece of twine from his pocket, he found a stick and tied the cat to it until his meditation was finished. After meditation, in keeping with his philosophy of respect for all life, the holy man fed the cat, which soon became a permanent member of the ashram. Therefore, in order to be like their master each of the disciples found himself a cat, and soon tying the cat to a stick before meditating became something of a ritual. This society for meditation, so the story goes, took the guru's name and continued in existence for generations after his death. But in the course of time the character of the society was subtly changed. After several centuries it was known as a society for the prevention of cruelty to cats. Of course there was a daily meditation period, and the philosophy of the founder continued to be the standard of orthodoxy, but it had lost its *authentic* character.

When we speak of movements or institutions as authentic we mean that they are true to their original prototypes in character and purpose. For example, a debate is going on today among the Hindu Swamis whether the Transcendental

Meditation movement as introduced into the western world by Maharishi Mahesh Yogi is an authentic continuation of the ancient Vedantic yoga of India. In the same way we can ask the question whether some expressions of Christianity continue the character and intention of Jesus Christ.

Unfortunately, there is no provision built into the historical process to guarantee that social institutions, whether religious, economic, or political, will remain true to the original intention and purposes of their founders. Even though an orthodox vocabulary is adopted and behavior patterns are codified, the character and purpose of movements are often subtly altered.

I have chosen the word "authentic" for the title of this essay quite deliberately, and I intend to use it according to its classical meaning rather than its more attenuated contemporary usage as a synonym for sincerity. Therefore, it seems necessary to begin with a brief explanation and definition of terms. What does it have to do with discipleship? And how does it relate to the mission of the church?

Authenticity and Sincerity

The word authentic comes from the Greek word *authentikos,* meaning *original.* For example, an authentic Rembrandt must be an original painting by Rembrandt himself. But more, it indicates that the "original" has a quality or character which marks it as truly belonging to the style of its originator.

When we apply this concept to organic life, we speak of a *purebred,* that is, a plant or animal that follows in genetic succession and reproduces the characteristics and qualities of the original parents.

When we extend the concept to historical phenomena such as social and cultural institutions, authenticity indicates that the organization or movement continues the spirit, character, and intention of the original founders. It need not be a *replica.* Indeed, a woodenly literalistic copy may be unauthentic because it has not preserved the quality which gives the original its genuine value.

Common today is the use of authenticity and sincerity as

full synonyms, but there is an important distinction which is significant for our study. Sincerity is a subjective psychological concept indicating an inner attitude of transparency. It means real or genuine, free from deceit. Authenticity describes a concrete form, identity, or quality which corresponds to an original exemplar. It indicates an objective, identifiable character. Thus, while it is true that the authentic item or person will have the quality of sincerity, sincerity does not guarantee authenticity.

The easy equation of the authentic and the sincere really stems from a presupposition of modern naturalistic individualism which does not recognize the existence of a normative original pattern for personal life. It does not acknowledge an original human prototype, whether it be an "Adam" made in the "image of God," or Christ who is called the "second Adam," "the man from heaven." According to this philosophy the marks of authenticity are purely subjective and individualistic because each individual begins as an autonomous and self-creating being whose future potential marks his or her uniqueness. Self-fulfillment is the criterion of sincerity or genuineness. Thus an authentic individual is one who is true to himself or herself. There is no authentic exemplar to which one should conform.

Such self-assertive individualism is affirmed with a flair by Virginia Satir in her recent book, *Self-Esteem: A Declaration.*

> I am me. In all the world there is no one else exactly like me. Everything that comes out of me is authentically mine because I alone choose it. I own everything about me—my body, my feelings, my mouth, my voice. . . . Whatever I think and feel at a given moment in time is authentically me. If later some parts of how I looked, sounded, thought and felt turn out to be unfitting, I can discard that which is unfitting, keep the rest, and invent something new. . . . I own me, and therefore I can engineer me.[1]

If the criterion for authentic human existence is not the autonomous individual seeking self-fulfillment, but rather an original person who has actualized the highest potential of all human individuals, then one arrives at an entirely different meaning of authenticity. Authentic in this sense, and this is the classical meaning, implies that the genuine model of personhood is to be found outside ourselves in one who is the authentic historical exemplar.

The Christian claim is that Jesus Christ is such an authentic model for human life and community; and our concern in this essay is to examine the elements of authenticity in witness to him which will give it persuasiveness and authority.

Authenticity and Authority

Authenticity, then, implies more than sincere, transparent, or unaffected individuality. Implicit in the concept is the notion of an original criterion or model which has an inherent quality of self-authentication, a model which has *authority* for us because it has acknowledged value and real potential.

A genuine authority is one that is intrinsic to us. Legitimate authority is the power of the authentic over us. It is, as P. T. Forsyth wrote many years ago, "interior but superior to the Ego itself."[2] By "interior" Forsyth meant that genuine authority does not exercise an extrinsic arbitrary power over us. We are not forced to submit to might, but are called rather to conform to a recognized right. As a power, the authentic is superior to the self, but its superiority consists in its being an authentic ideal—one that calls us to the real possibility of higher life.

Authentic power is the power to give life and freedom, to enhance and fulfill the intrinsic possibilities in the individual and his society. Especially in the areas of moral and religious authority, it is of the essence that this integral and necessary relationship be carefully maintained. Authority in religion does not depend finally on social or political sanctions, or upon personal attachments, but upon authentic power.[3]

Authenticity and Discipleship

The word authentic (*authentikos*) is never used in the New Testament. The basic concept, however, is contained in the language of discipleship. The Christ is not portrayed simply as God to be adored in pious devotion and served by a verbal proclamation of his atoning sacrifice, but rather as an authoritative exemplar to be followed in life and mission.[4] Jesus is called the "master" (rabbi or teacher), and his followers are "disciples" (apprentices); he is the "lord" (the one who had authority to direct), and they are "servants" (those called to loyalty and obedience). These are the categories that point to Jesus as the authentic model and indicate that his original authority continues in the church.[5]

The first Christians used words like *kurios* (sir, lord), *archēgos* (leader, founder), and *basileus* (prince, king) to indicate Jesus' authority in the church.[6] During his earthly ministry Jesus himself was called *didaskalos* (master, teacher) and *kurios*. Those who accepted his way were called *disciples* (followers, learners, apprentices), *Christians* (Christ's people), and *dedicated ones* (set apart to God, saints), to indicate their relation to Christ. And they were exhorted to "follow," "obey," "share in," and "imitate" Christ. We need to examine the significance of this language in more detail.

The concept of the master and his disciples dominates the Gospel accounts of Jesus' life. A teacher or rabbi in the first century was more than the supervisor or teacher of today's classroom. He was a person of great authority because he was considered a master, a model of excellence. His attainment through disciplined study entitled him to be an example and guide. His disciples studied his style as well as the subject matter in which he excelled, and they did this by literally following and copying him.

In this sense Jesus was called rabbi, but he was obviously a rabbi with a difference. He chose and called people to be his disciples. (The rabbinic students usually chose their teachers.) He broke with the "tradition of the elders" and assumed the role of an original founder who claimed and demonstrated the authority of God in his life and mission. His authority, in contrast to the other teachers of his day, was manifested in his exercise of authentic power (Mk. 1:22). When the legitimacy of his authority was challenged, he appealed to his work of healing, exorcism of demons, and forgiveness of sin (Matt. 12:28; John 10:38). By way of contrast the rabbis and scribes appealed to the orthodoxy of Moses, their Bible, for legitimization.

Nor was the unique authority of Jesus as Master attributed only to him in his historical role as rabbi. After his resurrection the major apostolic designations for him were "Lord," "image of God," and "Son of God." All of these stress his essential relationship to his followers as a continuing authoritative role model. As *Lord* he is to be obeyed; as *image* of God he is to be "imitated"; and as the *Son* of God he gives to those who accept his authority the "power to become children of God" (John 1:12).

The author of Hebrews speaks most clearly of him who is the "pioneer and perfecter of our faith" as our continuing example (12:2). He has this role not simply by virtue of the moral excellence of his teaching, but because he displayed the authentic character of God's life (1:3). Both John's Gospel and Hebrews use the word "glory" to describe this inner character. Glory means the inner radiance of genuine divine character. As one "full of grace and truth," Christ is "the Way, both the truth and life" (John 1:14; 14:6). He remains the authentic prototype for the church.

Those who accepted Jesus as the Christ were called his disciples. The implications of this much used word are little understood. A disciple is more than a pupil or student in the contemporary western sense of these words.[7] A disciple is an apprentice—one who learns by following, watching, absorbing the style as well as the intellectual system of the master. Disciples discipline themselves to understand and respond to life in a style that is authentic to the master.[8] In the words of Hans Denck, a sixteenth-century Anabaptist leader, "No one can know Christ unless he follow him in life!"

True, Paul did not use the words disciple and discipleship, but he expressed the same idea in his exhortations to "imitate" the Lord, and to "imitate [himself] just as [he] imitated Christ" (1 Cor. 11:1). To imitate Christ meant to have one's mind transformed by Christ (Rom. 12:2), to have the mind of Christ, exemplified in his incarnation (Phil. 2:5–11), to participate in his sufferings (Phil. 3:10–11), and to share in his mission as his ambassadorial representatives (2 Cor. 5:20). After an extensive word study, Michaelis concludes that in Paul, "the *disciple* . . . and *imitator* are one and the same."[9]

The other important designation of Christ's followers is *apostle,* which means *authenticated witness.* The word was first applied to the twelve apprentices to whom Christ initially delegated authority to represent him. Later it came to include a wider circle of witnesses, beginning with Paul and other first-century witnesses who in a special way were the continuing authoritative representatives. Finally, it has been applied to all disciples *as they have received the commission and Spirit of witness* to the original Word made flesh.

Perhaps to modern ears this language of discipline and imitation may seem literalistic and restrictive to personal development. The contemporary concern is to be "authentically oneself," that is, sincere and not a copy of someone else. In a culture where "I wanta be *me!*" even if I must ask "what kind of fool am I?" the discipline of following an ideal model seems to contradict freedom of feeling and expression.

But the New Testament concept is not literalistic, legalistic, or restrictive. Indeed, the message is that Christ came to set us *free* from restrictive traditions, taboos, and domineering relationships—the dominion of sin, and "principalities and powers" (2 Cor. 3:17–18; Gal. 5:1; Col. 2:20–23). To know and follow Christ, John wrote, is to be "free indeed" (John 8:31–32), because Christ did not issue a code either of doctrines to believe or rules to follow. Instead he bequeathed his Holy Spirit as the enlivening gift, and he invites us into the enabling fellowship of that Spirit. "Imitation" is authentic participation *(koinonia)* in the Spirit/spirit of Jesus Christ. It means identifying with Christ, not in mystical, private experience, but in the concrete sharing of his style, mission, and power. That is the pattern of authentic witness.

Christ's Witness and Ours

We have seen that Jesus Christ is the original authority for the church's life and witness. He is the authentic man, or as Paul puts it in 1 Corinthians 15:45–49, he is the "second Adam," the "man from heaven." In contrast to the rational "man of earth" who was chronologically first, he is the true original, the "man from heaven" because he is the "life-giving spirit." He is, to use another appellation of Paul, the genuine "image of God." In him was that quality of life and the power of life that marked him as authentic, and as the true image of God he is not only the "first-born of creation" but the "first-born from the dead" and the *beginning of the church* (Col. 1:16–18).

We must affirm further, despite a prevalent and influential dispensationalist interpretation to the contrary, that the witness of the church is in direct continuity with the witness of the Christ. Jesus as Messiah delegated his own authority to his followers so that they could continue and expand his witness to God's presence and power at work for the salvation of mankind. John Marsh has written that "Christ gave his followers *his own authority* to forgive sins (Matt. 16:19; 18:18; John 20:23), to heal diseases (Lu. 9:1), to expel demons (Mk. 6:7), and to proclaim the coming of the kingdom (Matt. 10:7–8)."[10] Indeed, one disciple recalled that Jesus had said that they would do greater works than he had done! That is why it is so important to understand the nature and ground of authenticity in the church's witness.

Jesus came to announce and inaugurate the rule of God for the salvation of mankind (Mk. 1:14–15). He did not come with promises for the future, but action for the present.[11] The very word "gospel," so central in our Christian vocabulary, underscores this present-tense character of the message and mission of Jesus. The gospel is news—public news announcing an event that has significance for the community. Jesus' mission was to announce such good news, namely, that *what had long been promised to the community was now becoming a reality in his own ministry* (Lu. 4:18; 7:22).[12]

The "rule" or "kingdom of God" which Jesus announced was not the explanation of a universal, timeless principle to which he was now calling attention. It was public news by which he was in effect initiating his mission. He was inaugurating a new era in God's creative self-disclosure in human history—the era of incarnate witness. His arrival was the event that made the crucial difference between the old era and the new. In his mission God was exercising his kingly authority (authentic power).[13]

As "the Christ of God" he exercised God's power for salvation by casting out demons, forgiving sins, healing the sick of body and mind, and forging the bonds of the new covenant community of reconciliation. Indeed, the goal of all his redemptive activity was the establishing of the new community of *shalom* (God's peace). One of the frequently overlooked miraculous aspects of his ministry was that he formed zealot (revolutionary) and tax collector (collaborationist), Galilean and Judean, scholar and working man, peasant and aristocrat, into a disciple community that not only survived his own untimely death, but became the dynamic base for continuing his mission.

Jesus' historical ministry culminated in his death on the cross and was vindicated by his resurrection. Indeed, in light of the resurrection the cross became the hallmark of his ministry—the authenticating sign of his mission. His ministry was that of a "suffering servant," a vicarious sacrifice, a self-giving leader in the struggle against hostility and death. Jesus himself characterized it as "bearing the cross" (Matt. 10:38; 16:24-25).

The early church enshrined its understanding of the significance of his death in the celebration of the Lord's Supper. They recalled the words of Jesus himself, "This is my body which is broken for you. . . . This cup is the new covenant in my blood" (1 Cor. 11:24-25). His blood, which signifies his total self-giving to God, including life itself, in their behalf, was the warranty or seal on the new covenant which incorporated the new community. Thus when the community celebrated the Supper, it was understood to be "a participation" (*koinonia*) in his body and blood (1 Cor. 10:16-17).

21

"He is our peace," Paul wrote to the Ephesian Christians, the beginning of the new reconciled humanity. He has effected a new covenant of God with the whole human family (Jew and Gentile), not just part of it; and he has reconciled us all to God *"in one body through the cross"* (Eph. 2:13–16). The phrase, "in one body," has double significance: Christ's one body on the cross was offered for both Jews and Gentiles. Thus he brought these two hostile camps together in one reconciled body—the church. This was his mission.

In affirming the continuity of the church's witness with that of Christ, we do not imply that he as the beginning of the church is simply first in a historical succession. In the same context that he is called "the beginning," he is also given the pre-eminence as "head of the body" (Col. 1:18). Christ's mission as the original Word of God is unique. He is the "mediator." He is the pioneer or initiator of the faith. In him God took the gracious initiative for our reconciliation. And further, God's initiative continues into the present! He keeps that initiative in his own hands through the Holy Spirit who is the true vicar of Christ. The mission is God's mission in Christ. When we use the Master/disciple categories, we must carefully avoid leaving the impression that we humans can finish what Christ began. He remains the Master—the Original.

With this clearly in mind, however, we are equally obliged to recognize that the mission of Christ was *inclusive* of us, not exclusive. Jesus called upon those who would be disciples to take up the cross, which epitomized his ministry, and follow him (Mk. 8:34–35). He was not speaking of "crucifying the carnal nature," but of accepting in fact his mission and lifestyle. Peter wrote that we have been called to a martyr witness "because Christ also suffered, leaving an example that we should follow" (1 Pet. 2:21). There also are a number of significant passages in Paul's writings which indicate that our participation in Christ's mission is a sharing in his suffering (2 Cor. 1:5; Phil. 3:10–11). He even speaks of his own concern and labors for Christ as "filling up Christ's suffering" (Col. 1:24), and of the church itself as "the fulness of [Christ]" (Eph. 1:23).

His mission as the Witness to God's salvation did not exclude our being witnesses. No, rather it includes and enables us to continue his mission (Acts 1:8).

Mission Belongs to the Witnessing Community

In conclusion, the messianic mission belongs not to individuals as such, but to the community of witness. This essential point has often been overlooked in Protestant circles where the mission was interpreted as a ministry of individuals to individuals with little or no appreciation for the centrality of the church. The church, not the individual, is the body of Christ in mission. Individuals are "members" of the body, and the "gifts of the Spirit" are entrusted to them as resources for the mission of the body.

According to Luke, the disciples were actually instructed to withhold verbal witness to the resurrection until the new community of the Spirit was formed as the authenticating context for their message (Lu. 24:48–49). In fact, not until the new people of God was formed as a community of the Spirit did they understand the nature and implications of their message. In the days before Pentecost their minds still turned to the restoration of old Israel as the community of witness (Acts 1:4–6). But, according to Luke, Jesus directed their attention away from a restoration of the old to the creation of a new people empowered by the Spirit (v. 8). That new reality of the church in the power of the Spirit remains the necessary authenticating context for individual witness.

Individuals received the Spirit of witness as they came into the new community (Acts 2:38). They spread the message as representatives of the community. They received the authentication of the Spirit for witness in the fellowship of the community (Acts 13:2–4a). They were "members" or "gifts" to the body fulfilling complementary roles in the mission (1 Cor. 12:27–31; Eph. 4:11–12). That mission, which has been given to the church, is to make known the eternal plan of God disclosed in Jesus Christ, namely, "to unite all things in him, things in heaven and things on earth" (Eph. 1:9–10; 3:8–12).

In summary, then, we have defined authenticity as correspondence to an original. In this case Jesus Christ is the Original Witness—the Word of God. We have argued that, according to the understanding of the apostolic church, he continues to be the authoritative exemplar or prototype for the church's life and witness to the gospel. However, that exemplar is not codified, but remains with us as his living presence through the Holy Spirit. We are not concerned with literal imitation, but with a sharing of his style and mission. And that mission is to expand the circle of disciples in authentic community under the new covenant. The authenticating principle is a new life of discipleship in the community of the Spirit.

Notes to Introduction

1. Virginia Satir, *Self-Esteem*, Celestial Arts Press, 1975, n.p. In the 1920s, when these assumptions of naturalistic individualism were applied to Christian theology by men like Gerald Birney Smith and Shailer Mathews, it was defined as what Christians at a given time and place believe. See for example Mathews, *The Faith of Modernism*, 1925.

2. P. T. Forsyth, *The Principle of Authority in Relation to Certainty, Sanctity and Society*, Independent Press, 1952 (2nd edition; first issued 1913), p. 270.

3. J. H. Schütz has persuasively argued that authority is grounded in power, which he defines as the "interpretation of power," that is, communicating and making accessible the power of life and freedom. This kind of authority is legitimized in its very exercise. As authentic power is made accessible to serve and expand the joy and freedom of life—to give that "eternal life" of which John speaks in his Gospel—it demonstrates an intrinsic authority which makes itself known in its very exercise. This is the kind of authority demonstrated in the gospel, which the apostle Paul called "the power of God to salvation" (Rom. 1:17). J. H. Schütz, *Paul and the Anatomy of Apostolic Authority*, Cambridge University Press, 1975, p. 14.

4. From the Reformation itself we have inherited a false dichotomy between a divine Christ, exercising his own exclusive calling to be a supernatural savior, and his human follow-

ers who could worship and give verbal witness to him but who did not participate integrally in his power or mission. It is understandable why this happened in their anxiety to disassociate the authority of Christ and the papal church. But it nevertheless has had unfortunate implications for the doctrine of Christian vocation and the mission of the church as an authentic continuation of that movement with Jesus Christ began.

5. *Authenteō* is used once in 1 Timothy 2:12 where the writer says, "I do not allow women to *domineer* over men." Apparently *authentikos* and its cognates were not used by early Christians to express Jesus' authority because they had become associated with domination and even murder. The despotic master *(authentēs)* had full power and authority over the servant to the extent of killing him. Note how the Roman Caesars commanded men and women to be killed for sport.

6. *Archēgos,* Heb. 12:2; *basileus,* mostly Johannine; cf. Lu. 23:2; 1 Tim. 6:15; *kurios,* dominant title. Cf. 1 Cor. 12:3. *Authentēs,* the cognate of *authentikos,* has come to connote despotic domination.

7. The *American College Dictionary* defines pupil as "one under close supervision of a teacher, either because of his youth or of specialization in some branch of study"; and disciple as "one who follows the teachings or doctrines of a person whom he considers to be a master or authority."

8. "The life of a [student in the Rabbinical schools] was made up of study of the sacred writings, attendance on lectures, and discussion of difficult passages or cases. Discipleship as Jesus conceived it was not a theoretical discipline of this sort, but a practical task to which men were called to give themselves and all their energies. Their work was not study but practice. Fishermen were to become fishers of men, peasants were to be labourers in God's vineyard or God's harvest field. And Jesus was their Master not so much as a teacher of right doctrine, but rather as the master-craftsman whom they were to follow and imitate. Discipleship was not matriculation in a Rabbinical College but apprenticeship to the work of the Kingdom." T. W. Manson, *The Teaching of Jesus,* Cambridge, 1963, pp. 239–40.

9. "The call for an *imitatio Christi* finds no support in the statements of Paul. But the idea of imitation as a mystical relation to the risen Lord is also to be ruled out. Fellowship with Christ certainly includes being made like him. But the passages in question make it plain that one can be a *mimētēs Christou* only by concrete obedience to the word and will of the Lord. Thus Paul does not speak of true imitation of Christ or God. His

reference is simply to obedient following as an expression of fellowship of life and will. The *mathētēs* (Paul does not use this word) and the *mimētēs* are one and the same." *Theological Dictionary of the New Testament*, IV, Eerdmans, 1967, p. 673.

Eduard Schweizer comments that the concept of following Jesus as a disciple seems to have been so closely related to following the historical Jesus that after the resurrection the church hesitated to continue using the term "following Jesus." But he adds, "the substance of what was meant ... remains alive, especially where the humiliation and exaltation of Jesus have also become important." *Lordship and Discipleship*, A. R. Allenson, 1960, p. 77.

10. "Authority," *The Interpreter's Dictionary of the Bible*, Vol. I, Abingdon, 1962, p. 320. Italics mine.

11. "The immediate present is the hallmark of all the words of Jesus, of his appearance and his actions in a world which ... had lost the present because it lived between the past and the future, between traditions and promises or threats. ... *To make the reality of God present:* this is the essential mystery of Jesus." Günther Bornkamm, *Jesus of Nazareth*, Harper, 1960, pp. 58, 62.

John Bright has also observed that while the kingdom of God theme was not new, there was in Jesus' teaching a "tremendously significant change of tense." *The Kingdom of God*, Abingdon, 1953, p. 197.

12. Paul S. Minear, "The Vocation of the Church: Some Exegetical Clues," *Missiology*, V, 1 (Jan., 1977), pp. 13ff. Minear gives a good analysis of "the specifications for good news."

13. See Norman Perrin, *The Kingdom of God in the Teaching of Jesus*, Westminster, 1963, pp. 187f. Commenting on Luke 17:20f. Perrin says, "... God is acting as king in and through the ministry of Jesus and his disciples," and the call is to recognize it as such. Cf. Matt. 12:28.

I

INCARNATION, THE PROTOTYPE OF AUTHENTIC WITNESS

INCARNATION IS THE FUNDAMENTAL PATTERN, THE prototype, of God's witness in Jesus Christ. The Gospel of John presents Jesus of Nazareth as the *Logos*, the Word, embodied in the human situation (1:1–14). "Word" immediately focuses our attention on the act of communication. God, John says, has always been a communicating God. *Logos* is the essential nature of God—"with God; indeed, God himself" (v. 1). God's primal act of creation is pictured as a communicative act. All "life" and "light" has its source and origin in God's Word, that is, his act of self-communication (vv. 3–4).

John further indicates that the communication is of a certain kind, namely, self-expression. J. B. Phillips' paraphrase of the first verse reads, "In the beginning God expressed himself." The emphasis in this case should be placed upon *himself*. As A. M. Hunter has put it, *logos* means "the ruling fact of the universe, and that fact [is] the self-expression of God."[1] *Logos* indicates God's creative yearning to embody himself in intelligent communicative form. It is the personal dynamic which is both actively engaged in creation and embodied in the living form.

The author of Hebrews addressed this same point when he wrote that God's creative self-expression, which in the past was glimpsed in many fragments of nature and prophecy, had reached its climax in the incarnate life of Jesus. Incarnation is the highest form of self-communication.

Paul uses the word *kenosis* (emptying) in Philippians 2:7 to speak of this communicative action of God in Christ. Christ, who was in the form of God, wrote Paul, "emptied himself." The meaning of *kenosis* has generally been analyzed in philosophical terms of human and divine substances or characteristics. What divine characteristics or prerogatives did the pre-existent Christ lay aside? But it is highly doubtful that Paul had such abstract ontological notions in mind. According to the passage the result of the emptying is that Christ became like us in our human situation. Knud Jorgensen has caught the central meaning and implication when he suggests that, in the terminology of communication theory, *kenosis* means that God "approaches us in our frame of reference."[2]

Incarnation, then, is the fundamental interpretative category for understanding God's mission to us in Jesus. All else in his ministry—serving, teaching, dying on a cross, and rising from the dead—is subsumed under the primary conditioning reality of incarnation! Who was it that preached the Sermon on the Mount? It was the Messiah, God's Son. Who washed the disciples' feet? The one who knew that "he had come from God and was going to God" (John 13:3–4). Who died for our sins and rose again for our justification? Jesus, the one designated Son of God by the resurrection (Rom. 1:4).

The *savior's* name is Jesus, which again underscores the point that incarnation is basic to God's saving action. Jesus, which is the Greek form of Joshuah, means "God our savior." The name marks his coming as a human infant, placing him historically and geographically. He came onto the human scene as any other human being—a man with a name given to him by his parents. It places him culturally, indicating that he was a Jew. As Paul wrote to the Galatians, he was not only born of woman but he was "born under the law" (4:4). The titles "Christ" and "Lord" were given to him because of his work. Jesus was his name.

Only as he was the fully human embodiment of God's

gracious purpose to save mankind could he be savior. The author of Hebrews is quite explicit on this point. In the context of a high Christology not unlike that in John's prologue, he insists that a full identification with us in the human situation was the necessary condition of his saving activity. He writes that Jesus took the same human nature as we in order that by dying he might destroy death. And he adds that "he had to be made like his brothers in every respect" in order to be our high priest (see Heb. 2:14–17). 1 John also insists on real embodiment "in the flesh" as a criterion of authentic Christian teaching (4:1–3).

Incarnation as Personal Life

To incarnate means to embody or incorporate.[3] It means to take on the full characteristics of, to be fully identified, or in solidarity with.

Embodiment has traditionally been associated rather literally with the actual assumption of "flesh" in the nativity, and theology has resorted to the philosophical categories of spiritual and material substance to analyze and describe the implications of incarnation. The terminology of the ecumenical creeds of Nicea (A.D. 325) and Chalcedon (A.D. 451), which has set the boundaries for "orthodox" theological speculation, is the language of philosophical discourse.

Such terminology is understandable in the perspective of history. Hellenistic philosophical categories were employed in the statement of Christian doctrine in order to refute heresies of a Hellenistic origin. This in itself was praiseworthy. But unfortunately, theoretical questions about the substantial (metaphysical) aspects of the incarnation have obscured the implications of the doctrine for the ongoing witness of the church. P. T. Forsyth has pointed out that most of the Christological theories "were fastened on the Church in the interests, indeed, of a true redemption, but at a time when the theology of redemption was apt to be conceived in terms of substance rather than subject, of metaphysic rather than ethic, of things rather than persons."[4]

It is unlikely that the New Testament writers had such

philosophical definitions in mind when they spoke of Jesus as God come in the flesh. Indeed, "flesh" refers not so much to a material substance as to the limitations that characterize the human situation. It graphically epitomizes the weakness of human nature. Vulnerability, dependency, contingency, need-desires, temptation, and death are all associated with flesh. James Denney was quite right when he observed that "the only incarnation of which the New Testament knows anything is the appearance of Christ in the race and lot of sinful men, and his endurance in it to the end. Apart from sharing our experience, that sharing of our nature, which is something supposed to be what is meant by incarnation, is an abstraction and a figment."[5] George Hendry agrees with Denney, and concludes that if the incarnation is viewed this way, "when we seek to interpret it we must use categories of history and experience and not merely those of nature."[6]

Incarnation means full identification with us in our human situation. When John says "the Word became flesh," he explains what he means: "he pitched his tent alongside ours"; "he dwelt among us" (v. 14). Jesus shared all the hopes and disappointments, the elation and longings, the joys and sorrows, loves and hates of his Jewish compatriots. Nazareth, a small town nestled in the low mountains just north of the plain of Esdraelon was *his hometown*. Jerusalem was the capital of *his country*. His life and destiny were bound up with this people and this country! Incarnation meant thirty years of cultural conditioning in a first-century Jewish community.

Perhaps Kāzantzakēs strained the bounds of historical imagination in *The Last Temptation of Christ* when he suggested that Mary of Magdala was the beautiful sweetheart of Jesus' youth, and in bitterness turned to prostitution because she felt rejected by him. But his impulse to picture Jesus as fully involved in the web of human relationships is correct. Jesus shared the everyday life of his family and community as any oldest son would have done.

This full sharing of our life is described in the New Testament scriptures in many phrases, like "born of woman, born under law" (Gal. 4:4), being made in the "likeness of sinful flesh" (Rom. 8:3), taking "the form of a servant" (Phil. 2:7; cf. Mk. 10:45; John 13:2ff.), being obedient to death (Phil. 2:8), "bearing our sins in his body on the tree" (1 Pet. 2:24). These are the historical and personal dimensions of the incarnation. The Apostles' Creed summarized them with the words "born," "suffered," "dead and buried."

Incarnation, viewed as a personal dimension of identification with us, indicates a quality and intimacy of relationship. It points to a degree of participation and involvement with us in our human life. Jesus was called "Emmanuel, God *with* us" (Matt. 1:23). In Jesus God *shares our life.*

But one must say more. In incarnation God shares his life *with us.* Jesus was "Emmanuel, *God* with us." Thus the very nature of the God who shares himself through embodiment defines the nature and extent of that embodiment. He is the loving Father-Creator who will spare no pains to bring his creatures back to himself. He is the "living God," the personal, self-communicating *Logos* who gives *himself* to us in life-giving encounter. In this personal *koinonia* of Father-Creator and person-creature we begin to glimpse the inner logic and dynamic of incarnation. Precisely and only in the full sharing of our life, can he fully share his life with us as savior. Incarnation is the shape of God's witness.

Docetism, Denial of Incarnation

One of the early and persistent heresies in Christianity is called *docetism.* The word is a transliteration of the Greek word *dokeō*, which means "to seem like" or "to think so." The heresy in a variety of forms rejected Jesus' full humanity and held that he only seemed like a human being. The ancient Greeks reasoned that a fully human incarnation would be a self-contradiction for God, who is absolutely perfect and transcendent. They were unable to conceptualize a fusion of the infinite and finite, of divinity, which is a perfect spiritual substance, with humanity, which is a corruptible material substance. In order to maintain the integrity of Christ's deity they formulated theories of a clear distinction and separate existence of the divine Spirit in Jesus.

The idea of God suffering was especially repellant to them. Gods might disguise themselves as men and act like men, but they could always escape suffering the consequences of human involvement.

But docetism stems not from ancient philosophical sensibilities alone. Its twin roots are rationalism, as we have just noted, and the deep fears and insecurities of the human psyche. If Jesus was fully human, not a superman of one sort or another, how could he be a savior? The cross, Paul observed, "is a scandal to the Jews and foolishness to the Greeks" (1 Cor. 1:23). A powerless, dying god is no God at all! A "messiah" who cannot deliver from the bonds of Rome must be an imposter!

Furthermore, docetism is not merely a theoretical problem in Christology, but a practical one in mission strategy. If genuine incarnation, that is, incarnation which includes death on a cross, is the shape of witness, then witness must indeed have the full meaning of martyrdom. All that Jesus said about "drinking his cup," "taking up his cross," and being blessed when we are persecuted must be implied in the martyr witness. (The root of the Greek word for witness is *martyr.*) One suspects that the docetic theological rationale, and our fear of a deep personal involvement that would make us vulnerable to suffering, are mutually supportive.

Docetic Christology has had at least three variations with counterparts in the way the church has approached the task of witnessing to the new reality in Christ. First there was the theory that Jesus was human in appearance only, what might be called the phantom theory. He acted as if he were human. For example, he pretended not to know everything, or he acted as if he were tempted. One might speak of this as the imitation of humanity in condecension to our weakness. He adapted to our weakness, but he remained strong. Only as the powerful one could he come to our aid. After all, it was argued, who would want to follow Jesus as Lord if he were a weak human being just as we are? The powerless want a powerful leader to save them. This is the strong underlying implication of the temptations of Jesus; and Paul refers to such feelings, as we have noted above, when he says that the weakness and death of Christ were "foolishness to the Greeks" (1 Cor. 1:20–25).

The counterpart in mission strategy follows the same line of reasoning. First, questions and objections are raised to a real incarnation of the church in a "non-Christian" culture, particularly when the cultural is still sacral in character. Indeed, during much of the period of Protestant missions, cultural identification with "heathen" civilizations was viewed as a contradiction of the gospel. Missionaries maintained Christian visitor status. Following political models, they set up small ambassadorial compounds of Christian culture and accepted defectors from the heathen religions who wished to transfer citizenship. They maintained their self-identity as representatives of an alien culture, and operated from a relatively detached position of power and financial advantage, adapting here and there to "native" standards.

We are not speaking only about geographically "foreign missions." One could just as well use "the other side of the tracks" for "native standards." Nor are we speaking only of historical past. One can still hear such a strategy justified on occasion by the argument that the poor, or natives, want a "gospel" that will improve their living standards, and a missionary example of the higher possibilities for material success—the ancient argument for a docetic Christ!

A second variety of docetic Christology has defined Christ as generically human, but not an individual man with all the limitations of a particular individual in time and space. His humanity is defined in abstract universal terms. The problem with this approach is particularly apparent when one thinks of incarnation in the categories of participation, personal relationship, and communication. Where is the locus of participation and responsibility for a generic human being? What universal vocabulary can substitute for the mother tongue? What timeless dogma speaks to the local needs?

The missiological counterpart to this docetic interpretation views the gospel as a universal doctrine, and morality to be transmitted by the institutional church. The institution

remains "generic" and relatively detached from local identification. Individual converts come into the church, the universal institution, but the church itself makes only minor
cultural adjustments to its local setting. Missionaries play
universally valid institutional roles, preach an objective universal message, and consecrate universally effective sacraments. The questions to which its gospel speaks are im-
ported with the mission, and it draws its answers from its
generic theological source which it assumes will fit all
human situations.

A third docetic explanation suggested that Jesus Christ
was part human and part deity. His body and psyche were
genuinely human, making identification with us possible.
The *nous* (spirit or mind), however, was not a human spirit
but the divine Spirit himself. The weakness and foibles of
the human Jesus were protected from error by the divine
Nous. He was tempted, but he could not yield to temptation.
He was bound by time and space, but, of course, he knew the
future. Thus he was theoretically vulnerable to mistakes, but
never actually made any. (There is no understanding of Hebrews 5:7–10.)

The apparent beauty of this explanation was that the
theologians could have it both ways: human participation
without human vulnerability. When the chips were down and
the contradiction of the cross was introduced, the essential
"Christ," who was the heavenly Spirit, escaped the final
results of human involvement. He was neither tempted by the
evil one nor did he die on the cross.

The counterpart in ecclesiastical organization is the distinction between and virtual separation of home church and
mission. The home church assumes that it can participate in
missions without fully entering into an interdependent relationship with the new believers. It continues its own self-
sufficient, independent life, sending representatives out in
mission. The missionary, who represents the home church,
in turn, never "empties" himself of the home church identity
and dependence. Rather he plays the role of *nous*, the protect-
ing, guiding spiritual intellect for the new believers. This is

mission without the ultimate involvement of a genuine incarnation.

The Extension of the Incarnation

Incarnation was not simply a temporary historical phenomenon. Once it had occurred, the historical possibility for relationship between God and mankind was raised to a new dimension of continuing personal intimacy. Certainly that is what was indicated by Jesus' promise of an Advocate, the Spirit of truth who would dwell with them and in them (John 14:16–17), and by the "baptism with" or "filling with" the Holy Spirit spoken of in Acts 1:5 and 2:4.

Incarnation was anticipated in "manifold fragments and means" (Heb. 1:1) before Jesus Christ. Then in him the focused character—"grace and truth"—of God was uniquely embodied in the human situation and became determinative for all subsequent embodiment of God's saving communication. But the ascension did not mark the end of incarnation with a return to the *status quo ante!* The Spirit of Christ came as the vital presence and authentic power creating the new "body of Christ," the community of the Spirit, which continued to be the locus of incarnation. Jesus Christ remains our contemporary.

Because the phrase, "the extension of the incarnation," can and has been interpreted in various ways, we must immediately make certain disclaimers. No institutional extension embodied in a "historical succession" of an ecclesiastical office is indicated. If we speak of the "church" as the extension, we must explicitly point out that "church" is not to be equated with denominations, that is, the empirical churches. John V. Taylor aptly points out that while denominational organizations may be a practical way to get certain kinds of things done, they do not exist as "theological entities." He continues with a most incisive observation:

> The New Testament uses the word 'church' with a number of meanings, but this [denomination] is not one of them. *When we speak of the church as an institution among the other institutions*

we turn it into one of the power structures, one of the principalities and powers, in fact; and it is from these that the gospel would set us free. The church can no more be an organized structure over against other structures than God can be an entity over against other entities.[7]

Further, the New Testament does not warrant speaking of an individual, whether in terms of person or office, as an extension of Christ's office or authority. Neither should we identify the contemporary extension of Christ's presence with private, individual "communion with God," that is, a religious experience or mystical relationship. Again, it is the body under the headship of Christ which continues to be the special organ of the Holy Spirit—the presence of Christ. Individuals as members of his body find identity with Christ through the *koinonia* (participation) and power of the Spirit.

How then shall we understand the New Testament concept of Christ's continuing presence and embodiment? Is it not through the gift of the Holy Spirit to the church? The Spirit is the agent of incarnation. The historical Jesus Christ "was *conceived* by the Holy Ghost." He was *baptized* with the Spirit's special continuing presence. And the same Spirit was the *enabling power* and *wisdom* for his ministry. Incarnation for Jesus Christ truly meant life in the Spirit of God. And he bequeathed that same Spirit to his disciples. Already during his earthly ministry they were given an anticipatory taste of his Spirit's authority over demons. Then, as the historical incarnation drew to a close, Jesus "breathed on them and said, 'Receive the Holy Spirit' " (John 20:22; cf. Acts 2).

George S. Hendry, in an illuminating chapter of *The Gospel of the Incarnation,* quotes Bishop Gore as saying, "It was pointed out that there cannot be more than one incarnate Son of God: but it is also true that what was realized once for all in Jesus is perpetuated in the world. The church is the body of Christ. It is the extension and perpetuation of the incarnation in the world. It is this because it *embodies the same principle and lives by the same life.*" Then Hendry comments:

> Only, this life, by which the church lives, *is not a 'principle'* that *the church 'embodies' in itself* in virtue of its historical succession, however legitimate that may be. The church is constituted the

body of Christ, not by the fact that it comes after him, but by the fact that 'Christ loved the church and gave himself for her' (Eph. 5:25), and it continues to derive its life from this source. . . . The extension of the incarnation then must be defined as *the presence of the Spirit in the church;* for the presence of the Spirit is the presence of Christ.[8]

The special work of the Holy Spirit is the creation of the new body/community and its empowerment for extending the ministry of Christ. That is why the church must be understood primarily as the *koinonia* or community of the Spirit. In a characteristically insightful discussion of the Holy Spirit as the cause and source of all communication, John Taylor calls him "the Ground of our meeting" and "the elemental energy of communion itself."[9] Further on he continues:

The Holy Spirit is the invisible third party who stands between me and the other, making us mutually aware. Supremely and primarily he opens my eyes to Christ. But he also opens my eyes to the brother in Christ, or the fellow-man, or the point of need, or the heartbreaking brutality and the equally heartbreaking beauty of the world. He is the giver of that vision without which the people perish. We so commonly speak about him as the source of *power.* But in fact he enables us not by making us supernaturally strong but by opening our eyes.[10]

This joining of communion (fellowship), community, and communication provides the key to authentic witness. More than twenty years ago Hendrik Kraemer pointed out that the greatest contributor to the breakdown of communication is "the social and spiritual crisis of today." Community, he said, must precede verbal language in communication. The fundamental problem is not to find a "new language better adapted and attuned to that mysterious elusive being: modern man," but to create "a common universe of discourse."[11]

Making a reference to Urban's book, *Language and Reality,* he continued:

. . . communication in itself, even if adequate, does not *create* 'community'; it presupposes community. So we could state the problem in the terms that there is a lack of community, and it is true that one of the outstanding marks of our age is a longing for real community, which constitutes true cohesion and participation of the same apperception of the value and purpose of life. With this key word 'community' it is easy to seize immediately on the key problem of the Church, which by its nature and divine purpose should be the embodiment of true community, as we know by the central place of *koinonia* in the New Testament as one of the new facts in Jesus Christ.[12]

The church, then, not as scattered individuals fulfilling vocations within the secular structures, and not as one of the institutional powers, but as small groups of awareness caught up in the new excitement of communion and communication, are the units of incarnational witness.[13] They are the dynamic components of a "common universe of discourse" created by the Holy Spirit for the ongoing encounter of God with the human family. Witness to God's salvation is the purpose of incarnation.

The Message of Salvation

Communication of the gospel of salvation is, as we have already noted, a personal or *self*-communication. The message *is* Christ, not doctrine about him; it is life, not ethical principles. The words spoken are words of introduction to Christ himself. The goal is not the mere transfer of religious information, but, in the words of Roger Mehl, a transmission of the presence of a "third"—a person.[14] Our words are words of introduction. The title of a book by Peter Marshall catches the intent: *Mr. Jones, Meet the Master*. The desire is for an *encounter* which leads to the *acceptance* of the Spirit (person) and style of Jesus Christ. The communication is a sharing of "Spirit and life," for it is the Spirit that makes alive (John 6:63).

The message, therefore, is already implicit in the person and personal style of the messenger. The disciple is the medium of communication. So Paul exhorted his converts to "walk worthy of the gospel." Authenticity, that is, the style of the Master, is imperative. Just as he came in the "form of a servant" and took on the "likeness" of those to whom he was sent, so the missionary community and each individual witness in it must take a servant role. And here we may speak of the communicator especially as the servant of the Word. So inseparable and interlaced are the message and life of the communicator that witnesses must share themselves in order to share Christ.

If communication by language is possible only within a community of discourse, it follows that the primal communication must be understood as reconciliation.[15] This certainly was the essential import of the Pentecost experience. The primal effects of sin were reversed. Clearly the stories of Genesis tell us that sin is an act of distrust which disrupts human community and causes distortion of communication. On that day of Pentecost A.D. 30, community and communication were restored under the lordship of Jesus, the Messiah. A universal community of discourse was re-established in which the fragmentation and frustration of Babel were overcome. "Every one heard them speaking in their own dialects" (Acts 2:6); and "all who believed were together and had all things common" (2:44).

This was the presence of the Spirit for which Jesus has commanded the disciples to wait (Acts 1:4–8). This was the witness of the Spirit, "the promise of the Father," apart from which speaking was ineffective. Communication as reconciliation, *koinonia*, happened through the uniting presence of the Spirit, "the Go-Between God." And Luke underscores this significance by noting that in each major extension of the gospel, to Samaria, Cornelius, Ephesus, this presence of the commonality of the Spirit was re-experienced in an observable way (Acts 8:7; 10:44; 19:6).

Perhaps no place in Scripture is this more clearly and beautifully enunciated than in Saint Paul's words to the Corinthian Christians:

> When anyone is united to Christ, there is a new world [of discourse]; the old order has gone, and a new order has already begun.
> From first to last this has been the work of God. He has reconciled us men to himself through Christ, and he has enlisted us in this *service of reconciliation*. What I mean is, that

God was in Christ reconciling the world to himself, and no longer holding men's misdeeds against them, and that he has entrusted us with the *message of reconciliation*. We come therefore as Christ's ambassadors. It is as if God were appealing to you through us: in Christ's name, we implore you, be reconciled to God (2 Cor. 5:17–20; *NEB* slightly emended)!

We have been appointed as Christ's envoys of peace sent to negotiate a reconciliation. Our service *(diakonia)* and message *(logos)* is reconciliation. And these are one! Language (verbal symbols), although important, is not primary in this message of salvation. Apart from the Spirit of peace and the environing context of the reconciled community, even the language of Scripture itself becomes the cause for misunderstanding and hostility.

How often, even when the language has been carefully selected, God has been misrepresented as a lawgiver and judge; "gospel" as a new religious system of beliefs and cultural values; salvation as economic and political power to control one's own destiny; and the missionary as a powerbroker, foreign agent, and policeman!

Identification, the Shape of Witness

The praiseworthiness of identifying with the needs and aspirations of those less fortunate than we is practically a pulpit cliché. And our often superficial attempts to be mindful of those who do not have enough as we enjoy our luxuries threatens to turn the very notion into a bland piosity, if not sheer hypocrisy. In some cases the term may conjure up negative associations of naive cultural adaptations or ineffective emotional involvement. And yet no other term that will carry the meaning comes readily to mind. Therefore we must attempt to be precise in our use of the concept.

Identification is the social analogue of incarnation. That is, in social relationship it corresponds to the philosophical and theological idea of incarnation. As a social concept it indicates an association of oneself with a group in feeling, interests, and action. It carries the psychological overtones of empathy, feeling for and with the other person. But the more specialized psychological meanings which imply a loss or transfer of self-identity are not intended here.

Attempting to define identification from the perspective of an incarnational model, we might well note that Jesus had a strong self-identity and sense of purpose as an agent of change in human culture. This suggests that identification should not be equated with an uncritical imitation of the host culture, which would in most cases be viewed as a loss of self-identity. Added to that is the fact that sheer imitation lacks authenticity. Neither should identification be understood as the simple adoption of "insider" roles. Although Jesus did adopt insider roles, being born into the culture, he found it necessary to break with common expectations as an insider. At this point our social analogy must be applied with sensitivity and prudence.

As an analogue of incarnation, then, identification infers an acceptance and respect for the other, ruling out paternalistic benevolence and unwillingness to be involved deeply in the lives of those whom we wish to serve. It includes *understanding* of and *sensitivity* to the patterns of social discourse (manners, mores) as well as *sympathetic knowledge* of the social structure of relationships. Further it means *appreciation* for the values of the receptor culture. The goal of the gospel is not to displace one human culture with another, but to introduce Christ, the power of God for the salvation of people and their culture.

Identification means *association* with the longings and aspirations of the people, and *involvement* with the people at the level of action to satisfy their legitimate needs and aspirations. Such identification with them must at the same time involve the people themselves in claiming their own aspirations and beginning to act in their own behalf.[16] Finally, it means the *adaptation* of life-styles to fit the values and standards of the local culture. Undoubtedly Jesus had this in mind when he told his disciple-evangelists to travel light and accept the hospitality of local families (Lu. 9:3–4; 10:3–8).

In a report to his home board, one experienced missionary to East Africa perceptively described the kind of practical situation which calls for full identification with the local culture.

The water system on a mission station breaks down. In the West we would do a feasibility study putting into the computer all the variables and constants and we would come up with a recommendation which would be accepted by everyone as, 'The best we can do given the circumstances.' But on this mission station there may be as many as a half dozen sociological groupings each with its own set of constants, variables, and vested interests. The missionary's Western solution is straightforward. He has looked at the intake pipes and sees that a simple, inexpensive change (requiring considerable manual labor however) would ensure a vastly increased water supply which at the same time would cut back on the diesel consumption of the engine. He represents the Western scientific orientation.

The maintenance department responsible for making the above changes, or any other changes for that matter, represents another sociological group. The chief mechanic, as spokesman for his group, recently had a lengthy hospitalization for a blood fluke, bilharzias, gotten from working in the lake. The mechanic isn't interested in going into the water again to make the necessary changes. So whenever he is approached about the problem he makes various excuses about the hippo breaking the pipes, etc. Another group is represented by the station treasurer who pays for the diesel to run the pump. His problem is that he must keep borrowing from other departments to pay for the diesel because some of the water users don't pay their dues. They don't pay because they aren't getting more than a trickle of water anyway. Since the treasurer has been unsuccessful in getting these people to pay, he would like for the system to collapse completely in the hope that the shirkers would be exposed. A fourth group is represented by the Training School director who is sure that if any effort to repair the sytem is made, his students will be drafted to do the manual labour. He certainly isn't going to volunteer anything, waiting rather to be drafted and preparing his defense against the likelihood of that unfortunate development. A fifth group is represented by the station manager who would really like a whole new water system paid for by government funds. The government has moved peasants into the area of the station and the peasants are using the station water, so letters of request have been sent to various government departments requesting a government water system. The station chairman representing yet another group feels that he had best just sit aloof from the whole mess. So for two years the station suffers with unflushed toilets and unwashed bodies while everyone asks everyone else whatever can be done about the water supply.

Now back to our missionary. If he doesn't understand the dynamics, about all he will do is get good and mad and nurture associated uncharitable thoughts. He will occasionally lash out at one of the groups involved in getting water to the station. After his outbursts the community somehow comes to the conclusion that the water problem is the missionary's problem and he becomes the scapegoat for all the vested interests that are keeping anything from being done. But if the missionary does understand the dynamics, he might be in a position to mediate between the various groups and maybe arrive at a solution. And if no solution is arrived at, at least he will know how to conduct himself in such a manner as not to antagonize the various groups among whom he lives and works. A missionary doesn't arrive at such an understanding overnight.[17]

Identifying with the other person is the initial act in creating a common ground of discourse. Three closely related principles help to elucidate and guide this process: *mutuality, dialogue,* and *vulnerability.*

Mutuality

The principle of mutuality states that an authentic Christian witness will do everything possible to communicate on an interpersonal and reciprocal basis. This immediately rules out all paternalism and any form of condescension or "talking down" to the other person. Thus the assumption by missioners that they represent a superior ideology and are donors of a superior culture, and therefore have nothing to receive or gain from the host culture, is unworthy of the gospel. One veteran missionary to Africa expressed it thus: "The assumption was that the 'Africans' would become like the missionary and not vice versa. We assumed that we missionaries would not change, but the Africans would. For a missionary to assume that the cultural trappings and loyalties he brings are part of the Evangel he preaches means that his adjustments to the mission field are minimal."[18]

According to the principle of mutuality, missioners will carefully avoid defining needs and goals of the mission from the perspective of their own cultural values. All systems of mission or church organization that place the foreigner in a dominant, commanding position will be seen as usurpation. All schemes of "development" and improvement which in fact create dependency upon the donor mission will be suspect. The ideal is interdependence, mutual burden-bearing and exhortation, and reciprocal sharing of the responsibility for the mission of Jesus Christ.

Dialogue

The principle of dialogue is merely an extension of mutuality in communication. It affirms that genuine personal communication can take place only in the mutuality of listening and speaking, receiving and giving.

Authentic witness must begin with genuine respect for the other person as *fully personal,* which is the psychological way of saying "in the image of God." It assumes that God has not left himself without witness in any time or place, and that the Holy Spirit, the "Ground-of-Meeting" who inspires all authentic communication, is present. Since human culture is simply the extension of the person in social relations, these assumptions clearly imply that every human culture has potential as a vehicle to communicate the gospel. Dialogue is the search for a common ground of discourse in which the gospel can be communicated.

Dialogue is not a technique or gimmick to gain the attention and interest of the other person, but an essential component of the message itself. Pierce Beaver has reminded us that religious systems do not dialogue with other systems. "Only persons who adhere to these religions meet and talk together."[19] Incarnation was God's person-to-person dialogue with us.

In a case study of Father Inocente Salazar's work among the Aymara Indians, Fred Smith elucidates the inner meaning of this principle. The "how" of evangelism, he says, reveals the "what." Then he explains:

The missionary has a vision that compels him to go and share it with others. He proclaims Christ through word and deed. His approach to the people, however, cannot merely be a strategy to bring the people around to a preconceived notion of his own regarding the Christian message. *How* the missionary relates to the people tells *what* vision he has of Christ. He is not merely an instrument who conveys doctrines to people, but he believes that Christ is alive today through his Spirit. A key difference manifests itself in the creating of relationships. Christ is not imposed as an object, but is a person revealed in and through relationships with other people. So the Gospel is announced, not just by word and deed but through personal relationships.[20]

Eugene Nida further helps us to understand the necessity of dialogue when he explains the "three-language model of communication" with which the translator often must work.[21] Our contemporary witness (or translation) of the biblical message cannot be equated with the biblical witness itself. It is at best a cultural translation interposed between the original and the new culture to which it is being presented. Thus there is at least a three-way dissimilarity between the participants. Nor can we assume that our own secular western culture is nearer to the Bible than are the cultures to which it is being introduced. When we recognize that some of the cultures receiving the gospel may in fact be nearer to the biblical culture than that of the missionary, it becomes apparent that the spirit of dialogue is fundamental to authentic witness. Indeed, missionaries from the West may receive much new understanding. This is what Fred Smith has called "the mutuality of evangelism."

Vulnerability

Vulnerability means forsaking our bases of power as we reach out to others with the good news. The New Testament enunciates this principle in many places. Jesus said that he was sending his disciples out "as sheep in the midst of wolves." They were to go without fear, depending entirely on the Spirit for their message. In answer to his prayer, Paul was assured, "My strength is made perfect in weakness." And however he impressed some of the Corinthians, Paul considered himself as their "servant for Christ's sake."

Of course, it is Jesus who most superbly exemplifies the stance. He "became poor that we might be rich." He emptied himself and took the form of a servant. He came not to be served but to serve. A servant claims no rights to self-defense and no priority of privilege. He humbled himself and became obedient unto death on a cross. The cross is the supreme symbol of vulnerability.

But what does vulnerability mean today? In short it means to forsake our power base of wealth and prestige, superior technology and living standards, and the protection which the political and military might of the United States affords us as missionaries.[22] We must let go of the notion that ours is the superior ideology to which all others must eventually bow. It means to put ourselves in a position of acknowledged dependence upon the citizens of the country in which we are sojourners. It means listening and learning from the people with whom we seek to identify, and making ourselves truly open and available to them. It means costly involvement in the needs and suffering of those around us. It means in summary to be "poor" in the sense that Jesus used that word in the Beatitudes.

As one surveys the history of evangelization through church history, vulnerability is a most neglected principle. We have excelled in translating and proclaiming the word, but have seriously failed to incarnate it in "bearing the cross." Pierce Beaver observed some years ago that:

> A century and a half ago our forefathers called oral preaching the "grand means" of mission. The word spoken by the living ambassador of the Cross with contagious conviction remains indispensable. Yet this writer finds more and more Africans and Asians who say that while the message is intrinsically good it is unconvincing. They claim that the lives, attitudes, and actions of professed Christians—even missionaries and evangelists—run contrary to it.[23]

Not only have we taken advantage of our foreign bases of power to maintain independence and cultural aloofness, we have actually presented the individualistic ideals of competitive initiative, material independence, and invulnerability as advantages offered by the gospel. We have offered the "wonders" of industrialized civilization as fruits of conversion.

Is not Jesus' refusal to do "wonders" precisely the refusal to take advantage of independency and power to accomplish his mission? He saw clearly that if he were accepted as a wonder worker—the giver of bread or the miraculous liberator from Rome—he could not be the savior. He had not come to preach the gospel of a reigning Messiah but of a "suffering servant." The taunting words of his persecutors ought to be the motto of missionaries of all times: "He saved others; himself he cannot save!"

Identification and Witness Roles

We have noted that identification does not necessarily mean adopting an "insider" role. "In fact," writes Jacob Loewen, "a reliable outside friend may actually 'get not only one but both feet inside the cultural door.' "[24]

It is important, however, as Loewen points out further, for the alien who wishes to induce change through witness to have a role relationship "that is valid from the insider's point of view." Otherwise, as a "non-person," the missionary who wants to be a servant-witness may simply be exploited and shunned. Indeed, a "non-person to be exploited," such as the tourist, is a commonly recognized "outsider" relationship role.

What kind of relationships fit an incarnational model? Loewen, to whom I am much indebted in this section, suggests three kinds of relationships for alien change agents: 1) the catalysts, 2) the friendly alien useful to the group internally, and 3) the symbiotic relationship.[25] Of these three, the second seems most inappropriate. It describes a relationship of continuing if not increasing dependence upon the alien power broker and the external source of supply.

"The distinctive feature about [the] catalytic function is that the catalyst is forgotten once the reaction has begun."[26] The missionary as catalyst is expendable. John the Baptist played this role for Jesus as he introduced him, and then moved off the scene. And in some of their brief contacts in

Asia Minor, Paul and Barnabas seem to have played such a role with varying results.

But the symbiotic relationship seems most significant for the ongoing mission of the church. The goal is reconciliation—the establishing of long-term, mutually helpful, and person-enhancing relationships under the lordship of Christ. This fulfills the social analogy of incarnation.

Summary

In summary, God's word of self-disclosure, his Witness, has come to us "in our frame of reference." In order to share himself for our salvation he shared our human situation, becoming involved in our lives as a genuine human being. This communication of God by incarnation sets the pattern for our witness of reconciliation.

Following his example with the enablement of his Spirit, who is the "elemental energy of all our communication" and the agent of reconciliation, our mission is to re-create communities of discourse in which the language of the gospel can be communicated. Identification, that is, fullest association with others in feelings, interest, and action, is the incarnational shape of authentic witness. Such a stance requires genuine respect for other cultures, confidence that every human culture can become an instrument for communicating the good news, willingness on the part of witnesses to forsake their power base and to build interdependent, mutually helpful and person-enhancing relationships "in Christ." This is only another way of saying that authentic witness is the appeal for reconciliation in behalf of the Christ who gave himself to reconcile us to God.

Notes to Chapter I

1. A. M. Hunter, *The Gospel According to John, The Cambridge Bible Commentary on the NEB,* Cambridge, 1965, p. 16.

2. Knud Jorgensen, "Models of Communication in the New Testament," *Missiology*, IV, 4 (October, 1976), p. 467.

3. The word "corporate" comes from the Latin *corpus*, which means "body." *Incarnate* is itself also from the Latin, meaning literally "to enflesh"—from the root *carn*, which appears in words like *carn*al, *carn*ivorous, etc.

4. P. T. Forsyth, *The Person and Place of Jesus*, Hodder & Stoughton, 1911, p. 331.

5. James Denney, *The Christian Doctrine of Reconciliation*, p. 242.

6. George S. Hendry, *The Gospel of the Incarnation*, Westminster, 1958, p. 95.

7. John V. Taylor, *The Go-Between God*, Fortress, 1973, p. 147 (italics mine). Howard Snyder makes an excellent analysis of the "church" and "para-church" structures (institutional aspects) in his paper presented to the Lausanne Conference, 1974. See "The Church as God's Agent in Evangelism," *Let the Earth Hear His Voice*, ed. by J. D. Douglas, World Wide Publications, 1975, pp. 327–28, 337ff.

8. Hendry, *op. cit.*, pp. 158–59 (italics mine).

9. Taylor, *op. cit.*, p. 18. This is in contrast to Tillich's use of "Ground of Being" as the proper term for God.

10. *Ibid.*, p. 19.

11. Hendrik Kraemer, *The Communication of the Christian Faith*, Westminster, 1956, pp. 82–83.

12. *Ibid.*, pp. 83–84. " 'Communication' implicitly confesses a given solidarity, taking one's stand in the world and as part of the world of the other, not over against that world, howsoever sympathetic this may be meant" (p. 61).

13. Taylor pleads that we recognize the normalness and normativeness of the "little congregations"—the "two or three" where Christ is in their midst. "But it is the 'little congregations' which must become normative if the church is to respond to the Spirit's movements in the life of the world" (*op. cit.*, p. 149).

14. Kraemer, *op. cit.*, p. 78.

15. John T. Mpaayer, Secretary for Translation in the Bible Society of Kenya, says that the word used in several African languages to translate reconciliation means "to make people hear [listen to] one another." Douglas, *op. cit.*, *p. 1233*.

16. William Glasser lists "involvement" as the first principle of "Reality Therapy." In *The Identity Society*, Harper & Row, 1972, he writes, "Involvement is the foundation of therapy."

The therapist, he says, cannot break the "intense self-involvement of failure by being aloof, impersonal, or emotionally distant. . . . Whatever time it takes, someone must break through the loneliness and the self-involvement to start a warm, intimate, emotional involvement where little or none existed before" (p. 108).

17. Joseph Shenk, "The Missionary and Community," mimeographed report to the Eastern Mennonite Board of Missions and Charities, 1975, p. 3.

18. *Ibid.,* p. 2.

19. R. Pierce Beaver, *The Missionary Between the Times,* Doubleday, 1968, p. 117. Beaver has an excellent discussion of "The Nature of Dialogue," pp. 110ff. See also John R. Stott, *Christian Mission in the Modern World,* InterVarsity Press, 1975, Chapter 3, "Dialogue." After stating the argument against dialogue, Stott argues for it, rightly understood, and he quotes the Uppsala statement (1968) as a definition: " 'A Christian's dialogue with another implies neither a denial of the uniqueness of Christ, nor any loss of his own commitment to Christ, but rather that a genuinely Christian approach to others must be human, personal, relevant and humble. In dialogue we share our common humanity, its dignity and fallenness, and express our common concern for that humanity' (Report II, para. 6)," p. 71.

20. Fred Smith, "The Mutuality of Evangelism," *Mission Trends No. 2,* ed. by Anderson and Stransky, Paulist Press and Eerdmans, 1975, p. 142. The document is also available through the Maryknoll Missioners.

21. Eugene Nida, *Message and Mission: The Communication of the Christian Faith,* William Carey Library, 1960, pp. 40ff.

22. How one should act in the complexities of each situation will need to be worked out with the local church. But clear disassociation with western military might seems clearly to be indicated!

23. Beaver, *op. cit.,* p. 11.

24. Jacob Loewen, "Roles Relating to an Alien Social Structure," *Missiology,* IV, 2 (April, 1976), p. 240.

25. *Ibid.,* pp. 226ff. Loewen's article does not seem to consider the possibility of a genuinely new relationship which should be expected to develop as the new community of witness grows in maturity. However, his delineation of "outsider" and "insider" roles is most helpful.

26. *Ibid.,* p. 228.

II

CONTEXTUALIZING THE WITNESS—THE DISCERNING COMMUNITY

CONTEXTUALIZATION IS A TERM OF RECENT VIN-
tage, but the concept and process are as old as the ancient
Hebrews. From the time of Abraham the people of God have
existed as a "movement" in history. The story of God's
people in the Old Testament is one of constant adaptation to
new circumstances. The story begins with a "wandering
Aramean" (Deut. 26:5) in the Arabian desert whose posterity
settled for a while in Egypt, then achieved a relatively short
and turbulent period of nationhood only to be scattered again
into the ancient cultures of Babylon, Assyria, Persia, and
finally in the diaspora of the Roman Empire.

In order to survive they were continually in the process
of contextualizing their life as the people of God. Yet some
how the vocation of Israel as "God's witness" (Isa. 43:10) to
the nations was maintained. Indeed, it could only be maintained in the process of contextualizing. Jesus rejected the
scribal "tradition of the Elders" because it had become inflexible and defeated the real intent of the original covenant
law.

The new people of God (the church) was conceived in a
period of extreme cultural flux; and although born of a
Jewish mother, it was weaned by a Hellenistic wet nurse.

51

The Christian community has always had to adapt, make changes, contextualize its life and witness, because it has understood itself as a missionary movement from its inception. For the young church, it was not simply a matter of adapting to changes that were inescapably imposed upon it by outside pressures. The new community initiated change in order to communicate its message of good news to the multiplicity of peoples and cultures in the Roman Empire. It translated its message, reconceptualized its theology, and adapted its religious customs. "I became all things to all men that I might by all means save some," said its greatest first-generation missionary.

The Bible as Witness

The witness of the people of God is closely tied to the witness of Scripture, and necessarily so. This has proved to be both a great advantage and something of a problem in the history of the church. The advantage has been that it gives us a continuing first-hand contact with the original witness. In fact, Scripture is part of that original witness. The problem has been how to understand and take it seriously as an authentic norm for the mission of the church without becoming literalistic and legalistic. In short, how to contextualize its message without adulterating its authenticity has been a problem of both theological interpretation and cultural adaptation.

As a first step in approaching this problem we will examine the nature of the Bible itself. Then we shall look at what is involved in the contextualizing process; and lastly, propose that the proper approach to the question lies in the authentic community of discernment rather than in orthodox theological definitions, standardized principles of interpretation, or a magisterial institutional authority.

First, we must note and take seriously the nature of the Bible as *witness*. The Scriptures are not a philosophical essay such as, for example, Plato's *Republic* or *Laws*. Both of these latter books are about the nature and proper organization of the human community, but are not historical works. They are rational dialogues dealing with basic metaphysical pre-suppositions, logical implications, and the political implementation of a just society. The Bible by contrast is a collection of historical documents. It records and reports the way in which God has worked with his people, gives poetic voice to the emotions of the community, interprets and theologizes about the meaning of the community's life, and preserves its accumulated wisdom. And all this not as a detached observation and comment, but as part of the ongoing process. The Bible participates in—is an authentic part of—the history of God's people. The Old Testament is the prophetic word given by the Holy Spirit to the living community of Israel. The New Testament is the initial fulfillment of Jesus' promise that when the Holy Spirit would come he would lead the disciples "into all truth" (John 16:13).

The Bible as we have it today was in the process of being written and collected into one book over several centuries, and actually exemplifies in its own production the process of ongoing contextualizing. Take for a first example the Law of Moses. Whatever form Moses passed on to his generation, it has come to us as a written document with many later insertions and editorial revisions which update, adapt, and apply the original covenant law to circumstances in later generations.[1] The changes from a nomadic life in the desert to a settled agricultural economy, and from a loose political confederacy to a central monarchy, are two examples of the cultural changes which required adjustment. Prior to the collection and canonization of the *Torah* ("the Law of Moses") it was the prophets as spiritual contextualizers who maintained the authentic tradition in the midst of changing cultural conditions.

The process in the New Testament is even more dramatic. Christianity was born in the midst of first-century Judaism. Its style, vocabulary, literary allusions, humor, theological categories, moral convictions, world view, presuppositions, manners, questions—all its cultural characteristics—were Judaic and Palestinian. Remember how the "Hellenistic" widows in the first congregation at

Jerusalem felt discriminated against.

Today, reading retrospectively, Jesus' command that his disciples should go into all the world seems obviously to imply a universal gospel. At the time it was not so clear that the message should be so adapted that it could be preached worldwide. At the first Pentecost the people who heard were Jews, either by birth or by conversion. During the first decades the Judaic Christians continued their attachment to the temple, and they were not at all certain that the message about the Messiah was for the Gentiles. Preaching to Samaritans and Gentiles were major hurdles which needed the special attestation of the Spirit.

Apparently Paul was the first apostle to catch the universal implications of the gospel. But by the end of the first century, Christianity was firmly launched as a Gentile movement, and the Jewish Christians who would not accept the culturally open stance of inclusion by faith apart from the Judaistic tradition withered and became extinct.

As the witness shifted from predominantly Jewish to Hellenistic audiences, adjustments needed to be made: Jewish ethical categories closely related to the taboos of "clean and unclean" were virtually dropped. The essential practice of circumcision was declared to be a matter of individual choice. Interpretation of and attitudes toward non-Jewish and non-Christian religions were re-evaluated. The sacral significance of pagan public feasts and festivals had to be reassessed. Changes in theological vocabulary and categories are obvious. Terms like "kingdom of God," "Israel," "Messiah," and "disciple" were largely dropped. Other terms such as *"ecclesia"* (church), "body of Christ," "conscience," "in Christ," and "fullness" became central. Paul retained some of his rabbinic categories and lines of argument to the end, but evidence shows that when he communicated with Gentile audiences he adopted their frame of reference and made use of their terms. He was thoroughly bi-cultural.

From our vantage point in history, these changes seem obvious and a matter of necessity in order to preserve the authenticity of Jesus' message. For Christians such as Peter and James, however, they seemed like things "hard to be understood." While they refused to break fellowship with Paul, as some of their more conservative brethren desired, they found it easier to simply divide the field of witness (the first comity agreement) than to fully adjust their own message to Hellenist Christians. To understand how serious and inflammatory these contextual changes were, we only need to recall that toward the end of his life, more than a quarter century after Pentecost, Paul risked his life and ministry in an attempt to heal the developing schism between the Jewish and Gentile factions in the church.

Our New Testament scriptures are the product of this turbulent period of cultural transition and contextualizing of the gospel. They were written in this matrix as interpretative accounts of Jesus' ministry, letters of admonition to new Christians, and timely tracts; and they reflect the cultural dynamism and pluralism of the situation.

The Authority of a Witness

To speak with precision, we must say that the New Testament is not a *single uniform* witness, but rather a *plural unified* symposium of witnesses. On the one hand we may properly speak of the witness (singular) of the Holy Spirit bringing the words of Jesus to remembrance; but on the other, we recognize the variety of human perspectives and situations represented in its pages. Its different authors bear witness in their own style, with their own vocabularies, and from their various viewpoints. And this plurality is essential to the authenticity of its unity. The New Testament has the quality of *authentic unity* but not of *orthodox uniformity*. This is significant when we recognize that authentic witness includes method and style as well as verbal content.

The New Testament is not an artfully constructed theology of incarnation with precise, carefully chosen, uniform, technical terminology such as one might expect in a theological textbook. It does not provide us with a glossary of correct terms which can be used as criteria for orthodox language. Its authors vary their style and adapt their vocabularies. They modify their approaches to meet the situations and issues.[2] We can easily observe this kind of adaptation in Paul's letters. In fact, the variety of style and vocabulary in the Pauline writings is so great that scholars vigorously debate whether all of the letters were actually written by him. The evident differences in the Gospels undoubtedly represent this same sort of contextualizing of the gospel.

We have spoken of the historical character of the biblical witness, but we must again be clear that the Bible is not a history text such as modern historians write. It is not even a collated, standardized report, but rather a collection of original, authentic documents from eyewitnesses to Jesus and his immediate impact in the ancient Near East. The New Testament exhibits a freshness and nearness to the original event, in sharp contrast to the detachment of a studied analysis. Luther had great appreciation for the "living voice" in communicating the gospel, and he correctly observed that the New Testament, even though it is written, shares the characteristics of living, oral witness.[3]

This unstudied, uninhibited variety of style and expression is far from a handicap in an original witness. Rather, it takes us a step behind theological and historical analysis which we moderns equate with objectivity, back as near as any written document could to the living historical personality and the impression Jesus left. It is an authentic extension of Jesus' own style as indicated by his use of parable and metaphor rather than linear logic, his easy adaptability in dialogue, and his directness in speaking to the immediate situation.

We have spoken of the New Testament compositions as original documents. By documents we mean more than written accounts reporting past events. They provide evidence concerning the nature of the events they describe because they are a direct part and product of what happened. Thus the New Testament is not merely a first-generation written report of what was remembered about Jesus. (Luke's Gospel is perhaps the nearest thing to a first-generation research report, but even it is so existentially involved in the events that it bears the character of documentary evidence.) It is one of the results of the resurrection and the baptism of the Holy Spirit.

The authority of the New Testament, therefore, does not rest simply on the accuracy of its historical record and the intellectual and moral credibility of its writers, but rests also on its authenticity and credibility as an integral part of the ongoing reality of the Spirit in the life of the new community. As documentary evidence of the continuing action of the Spirit enabling and authenticating the new community of discourse, it shares in and represents to us the authority of that original community of witness.

The authority of the New Testament rests on its dynamic relationship to the living community of witness. Apart from that environing context of authentic Christly reality its message, although intrinsically good, lacks compelling credibility. Not the verbal language of the apostles, but the "body of Christ" vibrantly and joyfully alive, convinced people of Christ's resurrection. Words have authentic power when they are spoken from within the environing context of the community of the resurrection.

If, then, we accept the New Testament as a uniquely inspired witness of the Spirit, must we not conclude that its mode of communication is more than a human peculiarity and weakness? The nature and quality of its authority is related to its *witness character*. Having emerged as an integral part of the witnessing church, it was accepted as *apostolic*. Is it not precisely this participation in the continuing incarnational witness that gives it authenticity?

We shall return to the implications of this for our contemporary witness in the last section of the chapter, but now we must turn our attention to what is involved in contextualizing the witness.

Contextualizing the Witness

In simplest terms, contextualizing the witness means "taking the context seriously" in communicating the gospel.[4] The term has been used in more recent ecumenical discussion to replace the older word "indigenization." Indigeneity is a biological metaphor. To be indigenous means to be native, to be born in or originate from. Obviously, a message brought from another time and place cannot be totally indigenous or fully emerge from the culture in which it is transplanted. But at its best, indigenization meant to become adapted to the new environment, to take root and grow in the new soil, and become a healthy part of the new cultural expression.

The problem with this metaphor is that it very easily implies too much adaptation and at-homeness. Taken to its extreme, it could mean that the only authentic "gospel" is one that originates within the culture, thus implying many valid revelations. Or it might imply an immanent message which does not challenge the sin and evil that are part of every human culture.

Contextuality is a metaphor from literature. Words have their meaning within a context, and as that context changes, so does the nuance of meaning. Such a context is in the first instance grammatical. Words have a variety of meanings in the variation of time and place.[5]

Thus, contextualization deals essentially with the communication of meaning across cultures or in changing cultures. How can the gospel message be made credible in its new context? How can it speak directly to the new situation as a relevant call to reorientation of life and hope in Christ? The concern is not simply to displace one particular culture with another, but to effectively call men and women to repentance within their own cultural context. At a minimum, the intention is to discriminatingly adapt the communication and application of the message to the cultural context so that "conversion to Christianity is coupled with cultural continuity," as one African theologian put it.[6]

The problem, however, is that adaptation of the message may lead to relativizing and syncretizing the gospel so that the authenticity of the biblical witness is lost. In America, for example, the gospel and the "American way of life" have too often formed an unauthentic eclectic synthesis. Voices in Africa and South America are proposing interpretations of the message that would form similar nationalistic syntheses of gospel and national or racial ambitions. Thoughtful theologians and missionaries are rightly concerned that contextualization might lead to what has been called a "chameleon theology"—a relativized gospel, and compromised witness.

What is at the heart of this widespread concern and agreement that contextuality is necessary in witness? Only a few decades ago the Roman Catholic church frowned on vernacular translations of the Bible, insisting that the liturgy be said only in Latin. While Protestant missionaries used the Scripture in translation, they duplicated their own denominational theologies and liturgical patterns. And they tended to identify gospel with their own cultural framework. Why the new interest?

First, we are far more aware today of the plurality and relativity of human cultures. We have come to accept and even value differences as complementary and enriching. Relatively few Christians think of their own particular culture as the only valid expression of God's mandate to the human family. *All* human cultures are relative to that mandate, stand under its judgment, and are potential carriers of the gospel.

At the same time, we are increasingly aware of the significance of culture as a system and carrier of meanings. "Culture establishes a common ground of understandings, a set of shared notions about how the world is ordered and how people ought, ideally, to behave."[7] Thus a people's culture must be taken with utmost seriousness if the gospel is to be meaningfully relevant. Further, culture is not static. People are constantly modifying, selecting, and re-organizing their systems. Thus a self-awareness and adaptation to changing contexts is important to communication.

Second, the emphasis in witness has shifted from speaking words to communicating a message. Protestant orthodoxy put great weight upon words themselves as the conveyors of the thought or message. Charles Hodge, following the philosophy of the Scottish Realists, said, for example, "The thoughts are *in the words*. The two are inseparable. . . . . Constantly it is *the very words* of Scripture which are quoted as of divine authority."[8] This concept of language attributed absolute and universal meanings to words themselves. Therefore it was deemed necessary to maintain key word symbols (theological terms) for an orthodox transmission of the message into any and every culture. Now that the relativity of language to culture is better understood, cross-cultural witness aims at the equivalence or correspondence of meanings rather than words. This principle also carries over into other symbolic cultural adaptations.

Third, with this new understanding of language and symbol, the nature of theological propositions, which are themselves symbols, and their relation to the reality of Christ and the gospel, is becoming clearer. Theology is a descriptive, reflective discipline by which the church seeks self-understanding in its cultural context. What does the historical reality of Jesus Christ and his good news mean for any given people? How should his life and message affect cultural understandings and practices? What does *metanoia* (repentance) mean in a given context? Broadly defined, theology seeks answers to these questions. Therefore its language must be contextualized in order for it to carry the equivalence of meaning across cultures.

Last, there is a new appreciation of the church as mission, and of the "missions" as "churches." Thus the younger churches have new impetus to accept responsibility for the ongoing witness to the gospel. If the younger churches are to carry their share of responsibility in mission, they must share ownership in the message. Christianity must be more than a resident alien in their countries. Christ must be incarnated in their own cultures in his body, the church.

What Dare Be Contextualized?

While there is wide agreement that contextualizing is necessary, there is much less consensus on what kinds of adaptations are called for. To say that the "gospel itself" should not be relativized or compromised only takes us to the root of the problem. How we understand "gospel" will in great part determine what dare be contextualized. The call is for "theology" to be contextualized, but how is theology related to gospel? Theology implies a broad scope of possible religious and ethical adaptations. How is the gospel to be expressed in human cultures? Can other world views be accommodated without compromising the gospel? Can, for example, African views of the high God, or Vedantic philosophy of the ultimate Mystery of Conscious Being, add dimensions to Christian theological understanding as the church discerns the meaning of Jesus Christ in these cultural settings? What social institutions and customs may be fully accepted, and what changes are called for as the dynamic of the gospel modifies a culture?

If we tend to equate gospel with a doctrinal system of propositional truth or world view, then a minimum of *language* adaptation is allowable.[9] One must maintain certain orthodox statements of "truth" in competition with opposed religious systems. If we tend to equate gospel with a sacramental reality embodied in an institutional religious organization, then minimal *structural* adaptations are allowable.[10] But if we equate gospel with the authentic *koinonia* (fellowship) of reconciliation to God and our fellows, then flexibility and openness to the grace of Christ and the power of the Spirit in each new situation are maximized. In that case, however, we must be clear about our touchstone for authentic contextualizing.

The *criterion* for contextualizing is Jesus Christ himself in his incarnation. He is the authentic authority, and as such he transcends every culture. Yet this transcendent gift was given in a particular cultural garb. That introduces the missiological paradox. Although the gospel offers a universal self-disclosure of God, it must continue to be offered in contextual particularity to be authentic.

The *guide* for contextualizing is the biblical witness to Jesus Christ which documents the historical event. This guidance, as we have seen, is given not as moral, legal, or philosophical principles, but as authentic testimony and exemplar—a living word in the midst of a responding community of obedience.

The *agent* of contextualization is the Holy Spirit given to the community as a spirit of discernment to lead it into "all truth." That community has been sent into the world, as Jesus himself was sent into the world, embued with the special energy and wisdom of the "Spirit of Truth." And that

Spirit directs the witness in relevant patterns of *agapeic* relationships, in intelligible language systems, and in credible communities of shared life and purpose. Christ wills to be contextualized, but on his own terms, in a body of disciples.

Aspects of Contextualization—The Living Bible

Contextualization is essentially a process of translation, and any translator of Scripture is immediately faced with all the problems, implicit and explicit, that we have touched upon. Therefore, one good way to put the question about contextualizing the witness is to ask, "Which is the *living Bible?*"

The complete title of the free translation by Ken Taylor is *A Paraphrase of the Living Bible,* but the abbreviated title which appears on the outside cover reads simply *The Living Bible.* Is the original Bible in Hebrew and Greek the living Bible? Or is it the vernacular translations and paraphrases? The question has been complicated in history by association of the living Bible with *authorized* translations such as the Latin *Vulgate,* the English *King James Version,* or the official Amharic version of the Ethiopian Orthodox Church.

The answer to our question is that the original Bible *was* the living Bible, and remains the living Bible only as it continues to communicate the authentic Christ and his good news to our world today. The Bible accurately translated into the great plurality of modern cultural contexts, that is, into the vernacular languages of the world, is the living Bible. Until its message is contextualized so that it can be effectively communicated it is not a living message.

This may seem obvious to us, but vernacular translations of the Bible have been considered highly problematic in the history of the church. One needs only recall the volatile reaction to Luther's translation into German, and William Tyndale's martyrdom for translating it into English. In our own day the strong negative reactions to authorized revisions of the *King James Version* indicate the continuing resistance. Only very recently has it seemed advantageous to multiply vernacular editions of the Bible. The Medieval church, by way of contrast, much preferred to make the "original" standardized text available only to clerics (priestly scholars) and let them give a "living" situational interpretation of its message in the context of a practicing Christian community.

This reluctance has been due in great part to the fact that even the simple translating of Scripture, which, of course, is far from a simple process, involves major contextualization of its message. Translation itself involves *crossing* cultures, that is, changing contexts. It requires finding correspondence of forms and meaning in cultures which may differ extensively from each other in physical environment, social organization, moral values, ideological perspectives, and forms of communication.

The translation process itself gives us some understanding of the extent to which contextualizing is necessary. The original event and witness was given within a particular cultural context. The "sources" (speakers/writers) and "receptors" (hearers/readers) of the biblical message communicated within a common cultural context for the most part. They shared a common background of assumptions, experiences, symbols, and meanings. Thus the message itself, in form and content, has definite cultural characteristics which cannot be simply transferred to another "non-identical" culture. Eugene Nida, in explaining the process, illustrates it with the transmission from a triangular culture to a circular culture.[11] The message must be reshaped so that the *communication* between the source and receptor in the circle is equivalent to that between those of the triangle:

thus $\triangle^{\text{speaker}} \triangle^{\text{message}} \triangle^{\text{receptor}}_{s \quad m \quad r}$ = $\text{(s)}^{\text{speaker}} \text{(m)}^{\text{essage}} \text{(r)}^{\text{eceptor}}$. Many adaptations in both symbols, linguistic form, and content are necessary for there to be correspondence of meanings across cultures.

Thus, already in the translation process we begin to be aware that a cultural incarnation or contextualization is needed in order to communicate the original message of Scripture across cultures. A translator who transcends cultural differences must at the same time identify with the culture into which he is translating the witness. Someone who is at home in both must interpret, adapt, and apply the original words to fit "non-identical" situations.

The witness of western missionaries to people of different cultures involves an even more complicated communication process because the translation/witness involves a "three-language"/culture interchange.[12] Here we may use witness and translation synonymously, since all witness outside the original cultural setting is a form of translation. The three cultures involved in this kind of witness are 1) biblical culture (Bible), 2) western religious culture (church), and 3) receptor culture (secular or other religious societies). This situation requires the witness to dissociate his/her own culture from biblical culture. The temptation is to equate one's own cultural translation (English scriptures, theology, and church organization) with the original biblical message and attempt a unilateral transfer.[13] Contextualizing means moving away from the familiarity of one's own frame of reference and joining a dialogue between the Bible and a third culture. In this situation one finds oneself in a position like that of St. Paul when he declared, "Neither circumcision [Jewish culture religion] nor uncircumcision [Hellenist cultural values] are anything, but a new creation!"

Interpreting the Bible

We have already seen that translation inevitably involves one in interpretation of both the biblical message and the receptor culture. It is itself an exercise in contextualizing the gospel. But as much as possible the translator tries to avoid theological interpretation. Theology is the task of the developing community responding to the original witness.

In order to allow an indigenous theology to emerge in a new cultural situation, we must begin by disassociating the concepts of authentic witness and a system of theology. This will mean taking a pre-theological and pre-institutional stance insofar as possible.

A pre-institutional stance in witness implies an incarnational approach, as described in Chapter One. We need not develop the idea further here, but only note that this approach is personal and relational rather than institutional and didactic. In identification with Christ, the authentic witness assumes the burden of cultural change, and seeks to make the gospel relevant and credible in a new frame of reference.

Our main concern in this section is with the implications of a pre-theological stance. The precondition for such a stance is an awareness that our culturally conditioned, theological interpretations of Christ are not to be equated with Jesus himself. Authentic witness is to Jesus Christ as he emerges in the pages of the New Testament.

An historical awareness of Christ, that is, an awareness of our historical and cultural distance from the Christ of the New Testament, is crucial to cross-cultural witness. We are probably in a better position today than at any time since the first century to view Jesus in his own historical Judean context as distinct from our own. Thus we are better able to make the distinctions necessary to dissociate him from the theological synthesis which is our "orthodoxy."

As recent as one hundred fifty years ago, most biblical scholars read the Bible as though it were written in and to their own century and culture. They did not attempt to understand its meaning first in the original cultural context as the writer addressed the Galatian or Corinthian Christians before they asked what it meant in their contemporary context. We have not even conceived that question clearly until recent times because we did not have the historical and linguistic self-consciousness to do it. Such self-consciousness is distinctly "modern."[14]

Today, however, this historical self-consciousness, along with wide cross-cultural travel, has given us the perceptions necessary to stand outside our own immediate culture and to relate the Jesus Christ of the New Testament more directly to the cultures in which we witness.

Contextualizing the witness requires a clear understanding of what theology is and how it relates to the original witness. Theology is an interpretative discipline which attempts to understand and apply the original witness of Christ in the context of the receptor culture. By nature it is a synthetic and contextual discipline. It attempts to present an integrated synthesis of the original witness and the present experience of a given Christian community in continuity with the historic faith of the church.

We refer to the historic faith as "orthodoxy," and use it as a touchstone for present-day interpretation; but the orthodoxy of one age does not remain a static criterion for theology, even in its own indigenous culture. Cultures differ in time as well as in geographical space, and one culture's orthodoxy must not be imposed upon another. Equivalent meaning is not the same as duplicate theological phrases. For the theological interpretation to have integrity, it must be an indigenous response to the original witness of Christ.

Indeed, the development of the various orthodoxies clearly represents the process of historical contextualization. Catholic orthodoxy of the early ecumenical creeds developed over a number of centuries, in an attempt to preserve the authentic message of Scripture in a cultural context that was in many ways foreign to the Bible. Protestant orthodoxy of the seventeenth and eighteenth centuries was an attempt to do the same thing within the context of the Reformation. Liberal theology was an attempt to recast Protestant orthodoxy in the context of nineteenth- and twentieth-century western cultural changes, and thus preserve its relevance and meaning for "modern secular man." Without judging the adequacy of any of these systems, we can recognize a similar process of contextualization in all of them.

The missionary, then, must recognize the cultural relativity of his/her own immediate theological heritage, and be willing to be detached from it. Detachment, however, does not mean rejection. Traditional theologies, both western and eastern, should be retained as secondary witnesses and be used in the full awareness that they are contextual interpretations. Detachment implies openness to let our theology be dialogically related to the emerging community's self-understanding in Christ. We should not impose our theological synthesis on other cultures as their orthodoxy. Authentic witness does not impose; it shares.

An emerging theology, then, should begin with the question of what Jesus, as he is presented in Scripture, means for the people to whom he is proclaimed. The task of the witness is to incarnate the authentic message of reconciliation in word and deed, and then to allow an indigenous theology to emerge in continuing dialogue with Scripture and the great tradition of the church.

Evaluating the Environing Culture

During the past two centuries, western civilization—Europe and America—has considered itself "Christian." Understandably, therefore, missionaries from the West to "non-Christian" cultures often equated their own "Christian culture" with the "gospel." In many cases they considered the "foreign" cultures demonic in origin, and thought it their duty to destroy and replace them. Few paused to reflect that originally the witness was given in an ancient eastern context that was in many ways nearer to African and Asian cultures than to the modern West. Working from this bias, western missionaries tended to see contradictions and discontinuities between the Christian message and the receptor "non-Christian" cultures. They expected the new Christians to accept the western cultural patterns as part of the gospel.

With the erosion of the Christendom ideal and the emergence of "free churches" in a pluralistc cultural context, this equation of national culture and Christianity seems clearly mistaken. No human culture has a monopoly on the gospel or on Jesus Christ. Conversely, all cultures have the potential to embody the witness.

On the other hand, culture is not a neutral instrument at our disposal to be used in communicating the witness, but a creation of human community that expresses the meanings and values of humanity in its sinfulness. Jesus Christ is both judge and savior of every human culture. The announcement of the good news of God's rule is accompanied with a call to repentance, which in every case has social-cultural dimensions. Thus the criterion for contextualization in a "non-Christian" culture is not a "Christian culture," but Jesus Christ himself the Authentic Witness who transcends both.

In its concern to contextualize the witness, therefore, the church must constantly discriminate in every culture. Today in the West the protagonist is secularistic humanism; in Russia and China it is atheistic humanism. In much of the rest of the world, cultures are just now emerging from sacralism, that is, a social order in which politics, morals, and social customs are explicitly derived from and express religious philosophy and values. Different national cultures are at different places on the continuum of change from sacral to secular. Japan, for example, has moved far toward a secular, technological culture, yet its funeral ceremonies, public political festivities, and holidays such as O'Bon, raise questions for the Christian community. Nepal is a Hindu state in which the king is also an incarnation of Vishnu and head of the religion. Pakistan, Bangladesh, and some of the Arab countries are, in effect, theocratic Islamic states. India's government is secular, but the transition from a sacral to secular culture cannot be effected quickly by legal enactment. The question is still debated whether India's culture is Hindu or Indian, that is, a sacral or religiously pluralistic national culture.[15]

Because cultures are not static, the church must be open to constant revision, restatement, and reapplication of the message. In societies that are adapting to secular, pluralistic influences, the church must determine when the secularization process has sufficiently eroded the sacral values and meanings of customs to neutralize their religious significance. Where cultures have adapted to the missionary message and have modified their own values and structures by assimilating aspects of it, the church must decide when indigenous thought forms and social practices can communicate the authentic message. In countries where nationalism threatens to subjugate all other loyalties and calls for the resurgence of tribal religions in its own service, the church must be on guard against new forms of idolatry and exploitation. In cultures where Christian values have been co-opted by secularistic and atheistic ideologies, the church must constantly discriminate the ersatz from the genuine and keep its own witness focused. Contextualization calls for constant and continuing evaluation and discretion.

These decisions must be made by the indigenous Christian communities as discerning bodies. Certainly what Petrus Octavianus says about Asian churches is correct and should be applied to the churches of every land and culture:

> It is desirable that not only individual Christians, but young churches in Asia themselves, consider and judge such matters with concern and urgency, seeing that the foreign missionary cannot do it for them! It will contribute to their growth and maturity to thus interact with their own culture(s), and, though the job be difficult and the process slow, to come up with results that allow them to remain part of their culture, but faithful and true to the Word of God.[16]

The Discerning Community

To summarize, I have argued that contextualization is an essential component of witness. Indeed, witness as a form of communication, in contrast to argument or debate, is a process of contextualizing or incarnating the message. Its stance is dialogical, not polemical. Message and method are inseparably fused. The ends are *in* the means. The goals are realized in the process itself. Only in authentic contextualizing can the original Word continue to be spoken.

Now we must turn our attention to the discerning community as the instrument of the Spirit to maintain the authentic witness. In a later chapter we will examine the community's characteristics and the marks of authenticity. Here we need to understand how it is grounded in the incarnation and continues that original witness. The community of witness is itself a cultural phenomenon and an agent for cultural change. Thus we begin by considering how cultures (people) are changed.

Cultural symbols, values, and meanings, as we have observed, are historical and relative. People change their customs. They alter social strategy and organization to meet new challenges to the community. Culture is not static. But what impels people to change their culture? Do intellectual *ideas?* Yes, when they come embodied as convictions of a person. Do moral *ideals?* Yes, when they come embodied in the engaging life-style of a community. Both abstract ideas and ideals must become concrete *events*. Cultures are changed by events that challenge the old patterns and call for new responses by the people.

Incarnation was such an event, and it has changed our history. God's self-disclosure did not take the form of an eternal intellectual idea which could function as a basis for a new universal theological system. Jesus did not announce that God has always been the creator and providential ruler of the universe—a rational theological statement which might be understood *mytho*logically or logically. He said that God's rule is about to begin—an historical (cultural) event which calls for active personal response.

Nor did incarnation take the form of a universal obligatory law which could function as the model for a just society. Jesus did not announce a revision or addition to the Law of Moses which could effect righteousness. He left a new kind of "law" which is not and cannot be a legal prescription—the law of love.

The incarnate Word was spoken as a relational covenant promise of absolute love (*chesed*, "loving kindness") in the old covenant, and as a personal embodiment of that love (*agapē*) in the new. Through the incarnation an eternal Word was spoken to the historical scene. The Word of reconciliation was *enacted* in the life, death, and resurrection of Jesus Christ.

The incarnation resulted in a new community, not in a new book of theology or a code of ethics. Jesus did not introduce a new principle or idea, but a new order—"the rule of God." The gospel was announced as an event which began and continues to change historical reality and meaning by establishing a a new community of meaning in the midst of the old. The Spirit of the risen Christ was given to it as its life force and self-consciousness. As the power of God, he motivates and enables for witness. He sensitizes the community to the alienation and pain of the world and arouses its compassion. As the "Spirit of Truth," he is the counselor and discerning presence guiding the community in its evangelistic mandate to be genuinely in the world but not of it. For better or worse, then, the community is the continuing witness to the incarnation of Jesus Christ.

The community does not proclaim itself, but is itself the witness (Acts 1:8). It proclaims the historical action of God in Jesus Christ, and his continuing present action in the Spirit. It does not depend upon its own words or works, but upon the primary witness of the Spirit in and through its life. And it points to Scripture as an authentic witness alongside of the Spirit giving a documentary record of the original witness.[17]

There is no substitute for an indigenous community of discernment in maintaining authentic witness. Apart from such a community the gospel becomes ideology. The verbal message of Scripture and preaching points back in history to the incarnation and forward to the consummation. But what holds these together and verifies the message as "gospel" is the present work of the Spirit creating the anticipatory community of salvation.

The gospel announces a new era, a new historical possibility. The resurrection marks the transition from old to new, and the church as the community of the resurrection must hereafter play a role analogous to that of the historical Word in Jesus. Like its Master, the church still "bears the cross," that is, it is an anticipatory realization of the final salvation. Nevertheless, the church is the living historical manifestation and witness to the reality of the resurrection. Without this continuing reality in historical form, the gospel is not "news" or "announcement." It is inevitably transformed into an ideology.

Thus the Scripture can find its proper meaning as witness only within a *community of interpretation*. Principles of interpretation are important, but secondary. There needs to be an authentic correspondence between gospel announcement and a "new order" embodied in community for Scripture to play its proper role as part of the original witness. The authentic community is the hermeneutical community. It determines the actual enculturated meaning of Scripture.

According to Luke's account in Acts, individual witness was delayed in the first instance until the new *koinonia* of the

Spirit was formed. The first witness was the formation of the new indigenous Jewish Christian community, and Peter's Pentecost sermon was preached "standing in the midst" of the disciples. It was the community, under the apostles' leadership, that interpreted the Scriptures (what the church now calls the Old Testament) as a witness to Jesus Christ, and the community under the aegis of the Spirit that decided questions of contextualization as the disciples spread the witness across cultural boundaries (Acts 15:28).

And so it remains today. The Bible, as guide and exemplar for authentic witness, can find its rightful place and function only in a community of discernment and obedience. "First of all [we] must understand that no prophetic word of scripture is a matter of one's own private interpretation" (1 Pet. 2:20).

Notes to Chapter II

1. Both conservative and liberal scholars agree that such emendations took place in the text. There are differences, of course, on how the process was carried out.

2. Harvey Perkins writes, ". . . contextual theology is not new. Rather it is the theological process of the biblical writers themselves. The struggle for contextual theology is to return to biblical style. . . . Take the interpretation of the Cross and Resurrection. It is interpreted in relation to legalism in Galatians, in relation to dualism in Corinthians, and in relation to issues of poverty and power in Philippians. Witnessing to the same truth in different times and circumstances requires us to state the truth differently. The Gospel is not a commodity which is packaged in one time and place, and then delivered pre-packed in every other time and place." "Issues of Contextual Theology: An Australian Perspective," *Ecumenical Review*, XXVIII, 3 (July, 1976), p. 287.

3. See Willem Jan Kooiman, *Luther and the Bible*, Muhlenberg, 1961, pp. 200ff.

4. Dr. Shoki Coe notes, "Either by accident or by providence we have used two words instead of one, *contextuality* and *contextualization*. I believe this to be providential. . . . Contextuality,

therefore, I believe, is that critical assessment of what makes the context really significant in the light of the *Missio Dei*. It is the missiological discernment of the signs of the times, seeing where God is at work and calling us to participate in it. Thus, contextuality is more than just taking all contexts seriously but indiscriminately." "Contextualizing Theology," *Mission Trends No. 3*, ed. by Anderson and Stransky, Paulist and Eerdmans, 1976, p. 21.

In my own use in this chapter I have not tried to make a clear distinction in the use of the terms. I have given them both the meaning Dr. Coe gives to "contextuality."

5. Bruce Nichols, who seems a bit leery of the term contextualization, defines it as follows: "The current ecumenical catch word is the 'contextualization' of the Gospel. This term includes all that is implied in indigenization but also takes into account 'the process of secularity, technology, and the struggle for human justice, which characterize the historical movement of nations in the Third World.' . . . Evangelicals affirm that the structures of theological interpretation can be indigenized but that the Gospel itself cannot be. Our task is one of communication." "Theological Education and Evangelization," Douglas, *Let the Earth Hear His Voice*, p. 637.

6. "To sum up, the quest for African Christian theologies, which has been vigorously pursued in the last decade, amounts to attempting to make clear the fact that conversion to Christianity must be coupled with cultural continuity. Furthermore, if Christianity is to change its status from that of resident alien to that of citizen, then it must become incarnate in the life and thought of Africa and its theologies must bear the distinctive stamp of mature African thinking and reflection. . . ." E. W. Fashole-Luke, "The Quest for African Christian Theologies," Anderson and Stransky, *op. cit.*, p. 146.

The spirit and point of view of Third World theologians generally can be seen in their "Statement" drawn up at a gathering in Dar es Salaam August 5–12, 1976. See *Occasional Bulletin*, Vol. 1, no. 1 (Jan., 1977), published by the Overseas Ministries Study Center, Ventnor, N.J., pp. 16ff.

7. Fred Plog and Daniel Bates, *Cultural Anthropology*, Knopf, 1976, p. 9.

8. Charles Hodge, *Systematic Theology*, Vol. I, Charles Scribner's Sons, 1895, p. 164.

9. In the papers presented at the Lausanne Conference on World Evangelization, one gets the impression that many authors assume that "supra-cultural truths of the Bible" are equated with

theological symbols and linguistic forms of language ("propositional truths"). Francis Schaeffer's paper, "Form and Freedom in the Church," e.g., is based squarely on the linguistic assumptions of Charles Hodge and the "Old Princeton" school of theology, which held that the thought is in the word. "Truth" equals an absolute verbal system of doctrine. He concludes that "the basis of Christian fellowship is Christian doctrine" (374). Thus their stance tends to be competitive, and they emphasize the incompatible differences between Christianity and other religious doctrines. This results in a minimal adaptation of "Christian" language.

In contrast to this, men like Bede Griffiths (*Vedanta and the Christian Faith*, Dawn Horse Press, 1973) understand theology as an analogical symbol system, and seek confluence of reality concepts behind the theological forms. Griffiths is particularly interesting as an example of this approach because he is interested in a dialogue between "orthodoxies," not a compromise or accommodation of liberal interpretations.

10. Howard Snyder's paper presented at the Lausanne Conference, "The Church as God's Agent in Evangelism," offers a stimulating and insightful distinction between the church and its "para-church" organizations which have too often been virtually equated with it. See Douglas, *op. cit.*, pp. 327ff.

11. Eugene Nida, *Message and Mission: The Communcation of the Christian Faith*, William Carey Library, 1960 (2nd reprint), pp. 33–61.

12. *Ibid.*, pp. 46ff.

13. René Padilla has noted that the gospel being preached in many mission stations around the world bears "the marks of the 'American Way of Life.' " One nation's culture religion has been transported to another. See "Evangelism and the World," in Douglas, *op. cit.*, p. 125.

14. The European artists of the fourteenth to seventeenth centuries painted biblical scenes as though the settings and costumes were those of their own time and place.

15. Contextualizing the witness involves evaluating cultural customs and practices. Does the *tilak*, the dot of vermilion which the Hindu priest puts on the forehead after worship, have religious significance when it is worn simply as a cosmetic ornament? Does offering incense at a Japanese funeral indicate "worship" of the deceased or merely respect for them? What about saluting and pledging allegiance to the flag? Is that different from bowing before a picture of the emperor? Should the festival of O'Bon, when the ancestral spirits are welcomed back

to the family hearth, be treated like Halloween, the hallowed eve of All Saints' Day? Does the Indian greeting of *Namasti* with a slight bow and the hands held in a supplicant position signify belief in the union of Brahma and Atman—God and the soul? One could continue almost endlessly with issues such as the meaning of marriage, the practice of polygamy, and foods dedicated to idols.

16. Douglas, *op. cit.*, p. 1242.

17. Moltmann quotes Käsemann from *An die Römer* as saying: "The gospel is more than merely the message actualized in the church; it is God's proclamation of salvation to the world, a proclamation not at man's disposal and independent even of the church and its ministers. This divine proclamation continually realizes itself anew in the proclamation through the power of the Spirit." *The Church in the Power of the Spirit*, Harper & Row, 1977, p. 388 n. 24.

This is a well-taken caution, but the major problem in Protestantism has been a lack of credibility because the power of the Spirit has not been evident.

III

INDIVIDUAL-IN-COMMUNITY— BIBLICAL PERSPECTIVES

In CONTEMPORARY AMERICAN SOCIETY, IT IS AN unquestioned assumption that the individual takes precedence over the group. "Freedom" is defined as individual independence. "Civil rights" means the individual's right to "life, liberty, and the pursuit of happiness." That the individual soul has "infinite worth" is a truism. Each individual must make his/her own free moral decisions apart from social coercion. Salvation and religious convictions are preeminently a personal affair, that is, a private individual matter before God. The very word "sacred" indicates for us a degree of intimacy related to the secret recesses of the individual self, and therefore a profoundly private experience.[1]

By the same token the community is conceived as a contractual association of free individuals. "Social" is considered the antonym of "personal." The concept of a "corporate person" is a purely legal construct. Indeed, the corporation and the social club (association) have become the conceptual models for community, and the only legal status of the church under the United States Constitution is that of a non-profit corporation. The concept of organic grouping has been heavily eroded by technology, urbanization, and ideology. Even marriage and family are increasingly accepted as matters of individual contract and convenience. The group has become for us a collection of individuals created *by* individuals *for* their own individual advantages.

In contrast to this, we have emphasized the community of witness in the previous chapters. The "body of Christ," we have said, not the individual member, continues the incarnation of Christ. The work of the Holy Spirit is the creation of the new community, and individuals receive the Spirit as they join in that *koinonia* of the Spirit. The end of authentic witness is reconciliation and creation of community under the new covenant. The community of discernment, rather than the individual, is the proper interpreter of the Bible as witness. It was the community under the aegis of the Spirit that decided questions of contextualization.

Such statements run counter to correct assumptions. At the least they imply that individuals have a secondary role in the witness. Does this not fly in the face of the great evangelical tradition of personal soul-winning? What is the place of the individual in community witness? How does one come to be a disciple? What does it mean to be an individual Christian? What does it mean to attain to mature manhood in the body of Christ (Eph. 4:12–13)?

The impact of modern rational individualism has been so overpowering in Protestantism that we must examine in some detail the assumptions and perspectives which underlie contemporary concepts of church and witness before we continue with the main theme. Individualism, as the public assumption or mind-set in America, has pervasively influenced biblical interpretation of the last one hundred fifty years. Particularly in light of the strong anti-religious bias of "scientific socialism," individualism has appeared to be the child and ally of biblical religion. In this and the next chapters, then, we shall look at some biblical and historical factors which can provide perspective on the issue.

The Biblical Context

Surely the Bible, especially the New Testament, affirms the significance and worth of the individual, but not all the implications which we have come to accept as "gospel truth" really stem from it alone. The truth is that we tend to read our Bibles in the context of twentieth-century definitions and assumptions, and thus we read some of these ideas into the Bible. If read in the context of its own historical and cultural milieu, the Bible challenges some of these assumptions. Modern concepts of individualistic religion and witness actually emerged during a long historical development and originate from a variety of sources.[2]

The problem of alienation between the individual and society, so characteristic of today's western world, is foreign to the Bible. The cultural background against which it should be interpreted resembles more closely some contemporary African cultures than ours in America. In these societies the individual is viewed as a particular embodiment of the organic family, literally tied to the ancestors as the continuation of their life force. The individual gains identity by assimilating into his/her own ego the identity of the clan. John Taylor explains this in *The Primal Vision*, giving us a profound glimpse into African views of man and religion:

> Man is literally a family tree, a single branching organism whose existence is continuous through time, and whose roots, though out of sight below the earth, may spread further and wider than all the visible limbs above. Death, it is true, makes a difference. . . . Yet in this single, continuing entity there is no radical distinction of being between that part of the family which is 'here' and that which is 'there.' A son's life is the prolongation of his father's life, of his grandfather's and of the whole lineage. . . . Man is a family. This living chain of humanity, in which the tides of world energy ebb and flow most strongly, stands at the heart of the great totality of being and bears the secret of creativity.
>
> The fact of individuality may often clash with the demands of this collective humanity, just as conflict often arises between father and son, and the occasions for this are far more numerous in these days. Yet the underlying conviction remains that an individual who is cut off from the communal organism is a nothing. . . . As the glow of a coal depends upon its remaining in the fire, so the vitality, the psychic security, the very humanity of a man, depends on his integration into the family.[3]

Viewed against this background, the significance of the biblical concept of the individual's relation to God can be seen clearly as a liberating revelation. The biblical view of individual responsibility before God in a relation that transcends ties to the community is the very ground of freedom. "For freedom Christ has set us free," wrote St. Paul to the Galatian Christians (5:1). And he continued by warning them not to submit again to bondage under the old tribal religious dictates that hitherto defined their self-identities (cf. Col. 2:9). But this does not embody the full meaning of modern individualism. Let us look a bit more closely at the biblical data.

Individuality in the Old Testament

Just as the presuppositions of humanistic individualism provide the working definitions and assumptions of modern western society, so the idea of group solidarity lies back of ancient Hebrew thought about mankind. We moderns assume that the individual is prior to the collective group, and that community is formed by a contractual arrangement of free individuals for their own mutual purposes. The ancients assumed the solidarity of the individual with the group. Mankind, as they understood it, is like a great tree with its roots, trunk, limbs, and leaves. Living individuals are like the leaves of the tree. They are ephemeral dependent units in the collective life of the ongoing social group. In such a view, based upon an analogy of nature, individuals' identity and significance are totally determined by the group. They have no personal independence or value in themselves.

Seen against the backdrop of this ancient tribal view, the Old Testament concept of the individual-in-community under the covenant of Yahweh emerges in its true perspective and significance. It clearly breaks with the nature analogy and presents a unique understanding of the individual in relation to God who transcends the community. This basic divergence with tribal concepts finds growing expression in the life of Israel as prophetic interpreters explore the implications of their faith in Yahweh.

Rather than attempting a thorough historical review of Old Testament and Jewish concepts of man in community, we shall give a brief resume of significant concepts which provide the background and basis for a Christian approach to the individual.[4] We must constantly remind ourselves of the importance of distinctive Old Testament ideas for our interpretation of the New Testament.

First, then, we must note that the primal human reality which is recognized in the Old Testament is the community—the corporate, social reality. As G. Ernest Wright has observed, the formation of community is God's central act according to the Old Testament. He writes:

> What to us and to most of the world's religions should be the dominant concern—namely, the life of the individual in his world—is in the Bible relegated to an important but nevertheless secondary position. God has brought into being, through redemptive acts which have culminated in Christ, a community in which each individual is called to participate. Individual and community are held together in a viable relationship without either being lost in concentration upon the other. Yet the formation of the community is God's central act. . . .[5]

It was with the community that God made the covenant—first with Abraham, father of the community, in whose "loins" it was believed the community already existed, and then at Sinai where it was renewed with the whole people who had come out of Egypt. Israel both in time and space was considered one community before God, and the covenant was primarily with the whole nation. Individuals were brought under the covenant of promise by being incorporated into the "commonwealth of Israel" through birth or conversion.

This view of the community as a primary and personal reality, in which individuals find identity through incorporation and participation, has been referred to by some scholars as "corporate personality."[6] The "people" or tribe is identified with its ancestor. For example, Israel may be the whole people or the ancestral father, Jacob. And likewise the individual Israelite has his personal identity as a "son of Israel." Thus he participated in the covenant as a member of the corporate person, Israel. "Throughout the whole period of the Old Testament," wrote H. Wheeler Robinson, "this covenant with the 'corporate personality' of Israel (as we may call it) remains the all-inclusive fact and factor, whatever the increase in the consciousness of individuality."[7]

Throughout the Old Testament, the worst fate an individual could suffer was to be cut off from his inheritance among God's people.[8] By contrast, the greatest blessing was to be completely joined to and identified with God's people in a festival of worship. Individualism could only be viewed as alienation. Personal fulfillment came through allying oneself with the life and purposes of the group.

Creation Stories

This view of the individual human being as a social person is clearly enunciated in the creation stories. According to these accounts the individual was made for community, as is indicated by a variety of data: 1) the use of the word *adam* for both the individual and mankind, 2) the concept of the "image of God" as relational (social), and 3) the content of the covenant. Let us examine each of these.

First, *"adam,"* which is predominantly a generic term for mankind, is used in both of the creation accounts to designate the highest creature which God made. It designates both *a man* and *mankind* (including male and female) in such a way that even when one man seems most obviously intended, what is said applies equally to all mankind. *Adam*, the first man/mankind, is representative, the arch-progenitor of the race in whom the race already exists. Thus it is the *human family* that stands at the pinnacle of the creation process, and not the perfected, rational, individual male of Aristotelian vintage. In the biblical perspective, the human family (community) living under God's covenant of peace *(shalom)* is the goal of creation. If this at first appears to be a negative point, that is only because rationalistic individualism has made the individual the epitomy of human evolution and value.

Second, according to the Genesis accounts, human beings in the totality of their physical-social being were made "in the image of God." To begin with, the image is not a special rational-spiritual faculty inserted or breathed into them, but a God-like characteristic of *adam* as a physical-social totality. It is not represented as a separate entity, a spiritual nature, added to the physical-social creature—an image of God *in* man, but rather as the imbuement of the creature with a spiritual quality, perception, or capacity which makes possible a unique relationship with God. It is not a rational nature which makes it possible for individuals to have a mystical knowledge of God apart from their social-moral relationships. It does not free the individual from the historical and social realms, but makes it possible for him/her to realize the transcendent dimensions of personal being through a "God-like" participation in them. The "image of God" is basically and essentially associated with mankind as *social creatures*.

Further, *adam* (mankind) is in God's image, and individuals express that image in their relationships as persons in the human community. In more traditional theological terminology, *Adam as progenitor of mankind* is in the image of God, and each person bears the image as he participates in *adam/Adam*. If this concept remains at the level of abstraction for us, then we have not experienced the profound reality of organic cultural community. But perhaps we can understand it if we say that it is not man and woman in their aloneness and alienation who bear the image of God, but the individual in relation—reconciled man/woman. Until the individual is in responsible relationship we can only speak of the image as a capacity or potential.

Lastly, concerning the "image of God" we note that it is immediately associated with mankind's ability to hear and respond to God's covenant. *Adam* is the *covenant creature*— the creature who in his/her very essence is a social personality. In the totality of his social-physical being he stands responsible under the covenant for his fellows and for the earth upon which he has been placed. Man received his unique personhood in response to the covenant which the Creator made with him, hence to fully understand the essential social nature of his personality we must observe the terms of the covenant.

The covenant which defined mankind's responsibility and, at least by inference, his nature, deals with his life in society and the natural order. The covenant gives the human family both a social and ecological mandate. Not only in the Genesis accounts, but also in the writings of the prophets, the point is explicitly made that the covenant is not concerned in the first place with special religious duties, such as sacrificial offerings and liturgy, which mankind owes to God. *Adam/adam* was to "subdue" (bring order) and have dominion under God over the earth. He was to name the animals and cultivate the garden. That is the ecological mandate. Male and female ("*adam*") were to multiply and fill the earth with their own kind. That is the social-cultural mandate. And these mandates were to be kept as a profound spiritual responsibility to God himself. That is the religious dimension which should pervade all of life.

According to the covenant, the goal of creation was a community of *shalom,* or in non-religious language a responsible, mutually supportive human society living in harmony with and as part of the ecosystem under the covenant of God.

In modern terms we may define *adam* as individual-in-community, that is, person. The Old Testament does not visualize human society as a collective of independent rational individuals who have autonomous individual identity, status, and rights apart from or prior to responsible social interaction. The primal reality is human community in which the individual as a participating member finds self-awareness and personhood. But personhood is not predicted as a humanistic base, either social or individual.

The biblical understanding of God as personal, and of his covenant as an absolute moral (not natural) law addressed to both the individual and community, provides the ground and definition of unique personhood. God addresses *adam* as one in his own image. In those ancient cultures that worshiped nature gods, society tended to depreciate individuality and submerge the individual in nature and the clan. Not so in Israel. Although there was a strong sense of the solidarity of the individual with the community, nevertheless individuals were believed to have a unique responsibility to God as persons under the covenant, and therefore they had a unique status in the community.

Consider how the following kinds of data infer this recognition of individuals and their responsibility before God: The people of Israel were formed not on the basis of blood, but covenant which implies individual response and submission. The *"Ten Words"* or commandments of Exodus 20, spoken directly by God, are given in the singular—*"Thou shalt. . . ."* They are not only spoken to the collective as collective, but to the individual within the group. Transgression of the covenant was considered not only to be against the community but against God himself. Collective retribution plays no part as a principle of punishment in the covenant as recorded in Exodus 20–23. Already in the Old Testament, love for God and the neighbor is made the ground and motive for obedience to the covenant law. Love is a highly personal motivation, and such an appeal could only be made to an individual.[9]

G. Ernest Wright has observed that in the Deuteronomic restatement of the covenant law there is an "alternation between the plural and singular forms of address" that is quite bewildering unless "both community and individual were constantly in mind." He points out that the community law of Israel was by no means a "tribal ethic," and he continues with an excellent description of the relation of the individual to the community order:

> Yet the individual was not lost or submerged in this community order. In it God's *'Thou shalt'* was characteristically singular, addressed to each individual. God's Word in the law singled out each person, so that as a responsible 'I' the individual heard the Word to the nation as being addressed to him personally. Man was not an insignificant and unsegregated component of a tribal mass. There was no such thing as 'mass society' in which the individual had no knowledge of himself, or of responsible selfhood, or of direct access to the sovereign power whose authority was absolute. In the covenant with the nation God dignified each member with his personal address, so that each one understood the responsible nature of his relationship to the Divine Person.[10]

We must make a distinction between individuality and individualism in discussing Old Testament concepts. The former calls attention to the individual as a responsible person in community, while the latter exalts the independence of the individual and his private rights. Individuality is affirmed in the form and content of the covenant; individualism is considered a matter of alienation and pride.

Mankind's sin is not the assertion of individuality in community, but the assertion of individual independence and self-sufficiency from God and his fellows. This point is made in many ways. *Adam* grasped for the knowledge that would give him self-sufficiency and self-gratification. "You shall be as gods!" said the tempter. The sin of the inhabitants of Babel was their collective self-assertion to make a name for themselves and to insure their immortality as a master race. Cain refused to take responsibility for his brother. In the days of Noah the earth was full of competitive violence. So the dreary story continued.

But in none of these accounts is sin identified as individual self-recognition of rights and responsibilities. Indeed, Noah and Abraham, the two patriarchs who represent new beginnings, are called as individuals to break with tribal identification and conformity. Contrary to some earlier interpretations which see the Old Testament materials as presenting a typical tribal view of human identity, these pages show a profound understanding of individual self-awareness and responsibility before God. At the same time they assume and idealize solidarity of the social group, and they show a high sensitivity to the sins which grow out of individualism, namely, unfair competition between weak and strong and the alienation and inequalities that result from it.

The Prophets and Psalms

The peak of individual religious and moral responsibility in the Old Testament may be found in the writings of the prophets. Indeed, the spiritual self-consciousness of the prophet became the prototype for New Testament religious experience. A brief glance at the prophetic consciousness is, therefore, important.

First, the prophet was profoundly conscious of himself as the servant of God under the covenant made with Israel. His essential message to the people was to turn from their sin and serve God in covenant relation. As one person under covenant, the prophet stood in solidarity with Israel. His confession for the people, for example, was spoken in the first person plural—"We have sinned." Speaking as the faithful representative of the covenant community, he calls them to peoplehood under covenant, not to an individual religious experience.

But the prophet was also conscious of a direct relation and responsibility to God under the covenant, which gave him the ground and courage to challenge the king, who was the corporate head of the nation. Indeed, this was the kind of self-conscious God-awareness that marked the authentic prophet. The self-identity of the court prophets was merged with that of the nation. They identified God's voice with the will of the national leader and spoke what the king wanted to hear. The prophets of the Lord, on the other hand, distinguished between the voice of God and national ego, and thus spoke as individual representatives of God to the nation.

The writings of Jeremiah and Ezekiel seem to reflect a new clarity of prophetic individual self-awareness. They prophesied at a time when the identity of the people as a nation was at its lowest point, and yet their solidarity with the community of Israel and their vision of the renewal of the covenant community are clear. The new spiritual awareness of individual responsibility before God did not lead toward individualism, but to a new understanding of the nature of authentic community in which the bond is neither blood nor law but the Spirit of God.

In his Lamentations over the fall of Judah as a nation, Jeremiah alternates between the use of the third person (they) and first person (we), and between singular and plural (I, we) in such a way that his individual self-consciousness and his self-identity as one member of Judah are simultaneously transparent. Even though rejected and persecuted by his own people, he views his own fate and that of the nation as inextricably interwoven: the nation's fate is his fate. Yet this same Jeremiah, out of his own sense of individual calling and inner certainty of God's word to him (Jer. 1:5–10), prophesied most clearly the character of the new covenant law that would be written upon the hearts of individuals so that each person would know the Lord for himself (31:31–34).

In similar fashion, Ezekiel, who speaks so forthrightly about the individuality of guilt and punishment (18:1–10), records his vision of the future resurrection of the nation by the Spirit of God (37:11–14) and of restoration of the temple which is a corporate symbol of religious experience and allegiance. Individual identity and corporate solidarity are equally part of his experience. The individual and the community are complementarities in his view of mankind.

The other major record of individuality in the Old Testament is found in the Psalms. Undoubtedly, we should not read the modern individualistic experience into the language of the Psalms, yet who can read the prayers of confession with their depths of introspection, or the expressions of lonely trust and confidence in God,[11] and fail to be impressed with the degree of individual self-awareness before God? However, in virtually the same breath the Psalmist expresses the solemn joy of solidarity with God's people in the act of worship, and the anguish of being cut off from Israel. The very meaning of the individual's life is represented as bound up with his participation in the corporate body of Israel.

In summary, even a sketchy overview of the Old Testament concept of individuality testifies to the wide divergence between rational individualism and the prophetic ideal. The idea that the social order exists exclusively for the mutual enhancement of individuals, and that political government is to protect their private properties, which has so dominated our own sense of both religious and political community, is quite foreign to the prophets!

Individuality Under the New Covenant

One of the striking aspects of Jesus' ministry was his concern for the individual person.[12] To him, the individual was not simply a specimen belonging to a class. He did not classify persons as Samaritans, publicans, Pharisees, fishermen, or Zealots. His choice of disciples exemplifies this, for they were a motley and widely divergent group covering the whole spectrum from Galilee to Judea, aristocrat to fisherman and farmer, collaborating tax collector to defiant Zealot. In personal exchanges he recognized each individual's unique self-identity and aspirations, and related to him according to his own inner longings and resolutions. He did not depersonalize individuals by viewing them as types.

Jesus' way of seeing others was not incidental or adventitious, but was related to his own self-identity as a unique son of God.[13] He clearly had a distinctive self-awareness of a relationship to God unmediated by priest or Torah. He had a sense of destiny quite exclusively his own, but that destiny bound him to his community in an original vicarious design of dependence and transcendence. His was not the self-awareness of a "Fuehrer" who relates as one unique individual to the masses. His own self-perception made him sensitive to the identity of each person, and his ministry offered to many the first recognition and acceptance of themselves as persons.

Jesus perceived his individual identity as a special relationship to God as his Father. (This does not come as a surprise. The story of man's and woman's creation directly implies that they came to know who they were only as they were individually confronted by God.) Like every historical individual, he achieved his sense of psychological and social personhood through interaction in an historical, cultural community, as the listing of his genealogy certainly implied.[14] His Jewish community was the conditioning matrix in which he experienced his spiritual self-identity, but this spiritual self-awareness as the Christ was given to him in a relationship to God that transcended the community.[15] The Gospel writers represent it as a voice from heaven at his baptism. And as he himself told his disciples, his true identity was given to Peter in a word from God and not from men (Matt. 16:17). His unique spiritual self-awareness as God's Son was received as the gift of the Holy Spirit—a gift he received "without measure" (John 3:34–35).

The possibilities for new dimensions of personal realization which are disclosed in the life of Jesus become the model (the *authentēs*) for all who will acknowledge him as their Lord. Just as Jesus' own unique personal identity was confirmed at the descent of the Holy Spirit when he heard the inner words, "beloved Son," so Paul says that we have been given the Holy Spirit in order to bring us to a full sense of sonship (Rom. 8:14–16).[16] Everyone attains the highest reaches of spiritual individuality only in the experience of transcending the social group. Our most profound self-awareness is attained in confrontation with Ultimate Reality, and in the Christian experience of individuation that ultimate reality is known as the Holy Spirit.

Speaking psychologically, this is the significance of Jesus' special gift of the Holy Spirit to his disciples as he left the historical scene. It was expedient for them, he said, that he go away so that the Holy Spirit could come (John 16:7). Their own maturity as individuals could not be attained in a continuing attachment to him as teacher. Only in a new transcending awareness of God the Spirit could they receive a new self-awareness—a new identity and confidence. The Holy Spirit would be their guide to truth. He would make possible a new intimacy of relation with God. He would give them authentic selfhood.

This new dimension of awareness and identity was anticipated by the prophets, and specifically foretold by Jeremiah and Joel. Jeremiah spoke of the new inward perception of God's covenant law (Jer. 31:33–34). Joel predicted the time when God's Spirit would be poured out on individuals of every age, sex, and class among God's people (2:28–29). Luke understood this prophecy of Joel to have been fulfilled at Pentecost when the prophetic self-consciousness became the common denominator of all those in the new messianic community (Acts 2:17-18). God's Spirit had created a new personal identity.

In the Pauline epistles the phrases "in Christ" and "Christ in you" denote this new dimension of personal identity. Instead of a self-concept formed through identification with Israel "after the flesh," that is, the old social reality, the new pattern is identification with Jesus Christ who represents the new beginning—the new Israel, the true son of Abraham, the "second Adam." The new self-image of

"Christ in you" supersedes all the old categories that deper-
sonalized and collectivized men and women. "In Christ" the
old categories of discrimination and prejudice are abolished
(Gal. 2:26–28; Col. 3:10–11). Every individual has been
given new dignity and status as a "child of God" and a
"member of his household." The new community is a community of new individuals.

Personhood in Community

We have said that Jesus gave new importance and dignity
to the individual, but we are not to conclude from that that
his mission was simply to rescue individual souls from a
future spiritual destruction. Jesus came to establish authentic community, and to this end he called individuals to new
spiritual awareness under the rule of God. His was not a
ministry of releasing individuals from the web of physical
and social relationships through inner spiritual enlightenment. (That was the goal of Lord Buddha, not Lord Jesus!)
He called individuals to new dimensions of self-awareness
and personhood in the new covenant community.

Jesus' self-awareness as the Messiah and Son of God
involved him in the most intimate identification with and
participation in his community. That is what incarnation
means! And the purpose of his incarnation was to reconstitute
the covenant community according to its original intention.
In the same way, the new identity of his followers as children
of God and participants in the messianic fulfillment involved
them in a *koinonia* under the new covenant which Jesus
initiated. *Awareness of one's new individual identity before
God inevitably and necessarily involves one in community.*
Life in the Spirit is a life of new openness to others in a
fellowship of reconciliation.

The new consciousness and appreciation of the individual's place in the community is indicated by the appeal of
New Testament writers to Abraham as "father of the faithful." The prototype of the new covenant is the Abrahamic
covenant and not the Mosaic. Both Paul and Jesus himself,
according to the Gospel tradition, appealed to Abraham as

the original, the *authentēs*, and to the Abrahamic covenant as precedent for their departure from the rabbinic tradition.

Of course these two covenants are not conflicting or even divergent in intent, but they do differ in historical circumstance and therefore in construction. The covenant with Abraham was made with an individual. In form it was a personal agreement without an elaborate code, which required from Abraham loyalty and good faith, and thus provided a basis for friendship. In the Mosaic covenant, the contracting parties are God and the "mixed multitude" that had come out of Egypt. In form it was a legal agreement requiring faithful obedience on Israel's part. Its purpose was the formation of a "people," that is, a national religious community. Thus while the Mosaic covenant was in historical continuity with the Abrahamic, it did not represent its fulfillment. A national community under a legal covenant (*Torah* or "Law") was not, and is not, the ultimate intention of the promise of Abraham.[17]

The messianic covenant established a community of personal relationship and loyalty based upon repentance and commitment rather than a legal-cultural one rooted in the biological family and its religious tradition. (Note how Abraham was called to break with his family and its religious tradition.) In both kinds of community the individual finds personal identity in community, but with a difference. Under the Mosaic covenant, individual identity was found "in Israel," that is, in identification with the religio-cultural tradition of the fathers. It was not merely coincidence that Jewish boys were declared "*sons of the Law*" as they were initiated into adult status in the community. Under the new covenant, self-identity is found "in Christ," that is, in identification with the Spirit of Christ who transcends the traditional historical community and its institutions even as he provides its form and dynamic.

Through the disclosure of the risen Christ as the living Spirit, a new perception of the interrelation of individual and community became possible. Christ as the Spirit became the formative principle (Word) and creative reality (Life) of the new *koinonia*. He is the light which enlightens everyone coming into it. Or in a different figure, he pours out the Spirit on each individual in the community. He is called "head of the body," and the community is said to subsist in him. Thus the individuals are related to the community by a relationship to Christ. They achieve their self-identity *in the community through identification with him.*[18]

This transcendent relationship gives the individual a new standing *vis-à-vis* the community. The new identity is not without the community. There is no more possibility of personal identity in Christ apart from the brother than there is of loving Christ without loving the brother (1 John 4:20). But both psychologically and spiritually a new freedom, a new quality of participation and interdependence, has been achieved in Christ. A new criterion of worth is established. A new definition of the person as "spiritual" becomes possible. And all this is possible only in community which is *koinonia in Christ!*

Authentic Witness

The biblical concepts which we have reviewed contain definite implications for both the role of the individual in authentic witness and the message itself. Although an entire chapter has been devoted to the shape of Christian witness, it seems appropriate to close this chapter with some further comments about these implications.

From a biblical theological perspective, individuals' new personal identity as Christians, or their new self-awareness as "saved" persons, is formed through identification with Christ in his body (community). They have witnessed (experienced) this reality, and now they are to bear witness (testify) to it. The individual, then, having found his/her own personal identity in the "new creation," the social reality, bears witness as a representative of the community. To be an ambassador for the national government one must be a citizen of the country. To be an "ambassador for Christ," who is Lord of the new community, necessarily involves one in responsible participation and representation of that community.

The message of good news is the announcement of the new covenant community being formed in Christ—a community of the Spirit in which one finds true personal fulfillment and freedom. The witness is to this new reality which has been formed in Christ. The evangelistic call is to *repent*, that is, to turn from the independency, self-sufficiency, and pride that characterize human beings in their alienation, and to submit to the new Lord under covenant in authentic *koinonia*. The authentic biblical pattern of witness, therefore, is not one detached individual leading another one to a "private" religious experience with a disincarnate, spiritual Christ who may be known separately from his body.

Now, of course, this does not mean that the individual can never witness in geographical detachment from the group. Community responsibility and personal relationship are not matters of simple physical presence. And geographical separation is not only allowable but necessary for the spread of the good news. Participation in community is, to some degree, a matter of faithfulness to the message of Scripture as understood in the apostolic ecumenical tradition of the church. In part it is a matter of fellowship and accountability to an acknowledged Christian fellowship. And, perhaps most importantly, it is in large part a matter of authentic demonstration of covenant relationship in the community of salvation that forms as a response to witness. "Let each take care how he builds," Paul warned the Corinthian evangelists. The only "foundation" is Christ, and the "temple" they are building is God's holy community where the Spirit of God dwells (1 Cor. 3:10–17).

Notes to Chapter III

1. This individualistic religious stance is vividly portrayed in the idealized body language of Protestant worship. Individual wor-

shipers are seated in long rows with heads bowed, eyes closed, and hands clasped in silent reverence before God in the church of their choice.

2. For a number of reasons growing out of historical circumstances in the last century, this issue of the individual in community has become a highly sensitive one for conservative American Protestants. Terms like "Social Gospel," socialism, communalism, and especially communism immediately raise objections. Perhaps for this reason it would be advisable for me to repeat that I have no design in this chapter to defend any political system by the Bible. In any case, Communism as it has developed in Russia and Eastern Europe represents a "collectivization," not an organic community. Neither do I espouse the liberal "Social Gospel" of the early twentieth century, although I do believe that there are social dimensions to the gospel that have been overlooked and neglected in conservative Protestantism.

3. John V. Taylor, *The Primal Vision*, SCM, 1963, pp. 99f.

4. For extended studies of the biblical doctrine of man see the following: Walther Eichrodt, *Man in the Old Testament*, Alec R. Allenson, 1951; E. F. Scott, *Man and Society in the New Testament*, Scribners, 1947; Russell Shedd, *Man in Community*, Eerdmans, 1964; and G. Ernest Wright, *The Biblical Doctrine of Man in Society*, SCM, 1954.

5. Wright, *op. cit.*, pp. 18f.

6. The concept of "corporate personality" was introduced into Old Testament studies by the famous Baptist scholar, H. Wheeler Robinson, in the early part of this century. See his *Christian Doctrine of Man*, and articles like "Corporate Personality in Ancient Israel" (1935), and "The Group and the Individual in Ancient Israel" (1937). More recently this idea has been sharply challenged by some biblical scholars. See, for example, G. E. Mendenhall, "The Relation of the Individual to Political Society in Ancient Israel," *Biblical Studies in Memory of H. C. Alleman*, ed. by J. M. Myers, J. J. Augustin Publishers, 1960; J. R. Porter, "The Legal Aspects of the Concept of 'Corporate Personality' in the Old Testament," *Vetus Testamentum*, XI (July, 1965), pp. 361–80; and J. W. Rogerson, "The Hebrew Conception of Corporate Personality: A Re-examination," *Journal of Theological Studies*, XXI (April, 1970), pp. 1–16.

7. Robinson, *Corporate Personality in Ancient Israel*, Fortress (Facet Book), 1964, pp. 26–27.

8. In a similar fashion, the Japanese phrases *jibun no aru* and *jibun no nai* speak of individuals having or lacking a self-

identity, depending on their relation to the family or clan unit. One who has been ostracized has lost selfhood. See Takeo Doi, *The Anatomy of Dependence*, Harper & Row, 1973, pp. 132ff.

9. See Eichrodt, *op. cit.*, pp. 13ff., for an extended discussion of this material.

10. Wright, *op. cit.*, pp. 25f.

11. See, for example, Ps. 32:3–5; 62:1–2.

12. E. F. Scott, in *Man and Society in the New Testament,* held that "It was Jesus who first discovered that every man is a person, with value and destiny of his own" (p. 83). This seems to be too strong a statement of the point in light of our own review of the Old Testament materials. Scott's liberal individualistic bias seems to be showing.

13. I do not intend here any negative assessment of Jesus' status as Son of God. That is a theological issue and at the moment I am attempting to make a psychological point.

14. Matt. 1:1–16; Lu. 3:23–38. Cf. Paul's description of him as "born of woman, *born under the Law*" in Gal. 4:4.

15. It is unthinkable that Jesus could have come to self-consciousness as the "Messiah" outside the Jewish community. It was his cultural context that made his experience of identity crisis and resolution quite distinct from the "enlightenment" of the Buddha, for example.

16. Paul applies the metaphor of sonship to all believers, male and female. In first-century culture it was the sons who had legal family status—freedom and inheritance—and it is this sonship status which belongs now to all in God's family.

17. The unavoidable implication of dispensationalist theology, which makes a Jewish, Palestinian kingdom the final historical goal of the Messiah and the fulfillment of the Abrahamic covenant, is that *law* and *nationalism* are God's final words in history! The kingdom of God on earth becomes a universal messianic political system administered under a "rule of iron."

18. While this relation to the community is not formally different from the Jew's relation through identification as a "son of the Law," the radical difference lies in the fact that law cannot transcend community in the way a living person does. The prophetic experience is the precursor of the new relationship. In the name of Yahweh the prophet challenged the community's understanding and use of the law.

IV

INDIVIDUAL AND COMMUNITY—HISTORICAL DEVELOPMENTS

THE THEOLOGICAL SYNTHESIS OF BIBLICAL AND Aristotelian ideas which lies back of contemporary evangelical Protestantism represents a step forward in the understanding of individual freedom and responsibility. At best it is a genuine extension of biblical personalism. However, it also contains implicit assumptions and concepts which in their development have actually undercut evangelical witness to authentic community under the rule of God. Partly as an historical reaction to Marxist materialism and other varieties of naturalism, and partly as a logical consequence of its own theological definitions, American evangelicalism has been the champion of individualistic religion.[1]

This chapter will attempt to unscramble some of the definitions, assumptions, and social movements that inform contemporary Protestant evangelicalism, and examine their effects on the formulation of evangelical doctrines of salvation and witness. First we shall examine roots and developments in the history of individualism. Then we will turn to its influence and effects on Christian beliefs and experience.

Ancient Roots

The New Testament witness to a "new creation" of the individual in Christ is one root of modern individualism's assertion that the individual takes precedence over the group. However, as I have attempted to show, the two can by no means be equated. To read individualistic religion into Scripture is an anachronism. The New Testament does not provide a new metaphysical base by divinizing man, as Ernst Troeltsch suggested.[2] Neither does it provide a justification for idealizing the autonomous competitive individual. To be in Christ is to be in solidarity with him through participation in his body. The new being is individual-in-authentic-community.

The other root of modern individualism is the Graeco-Roman philosophical tradition, which grounded the individual's human identity in his (and not her) "rational" capacity. The tradition is clearly traceable to Aristotle's idealization of the self-sufficient philosopher. It reaches its peak of idealism in the Stoics of the first century B.C., who conceived of the individual, at least the male individual, as a spark of the divine universal Reason. That spark shines brighter in some than in others, but it exists in all. "Remember who you are" is the exhortation of the Stoic, Epictetus, to his country-men. But this tradition was elitist from Aristotle to Marcus Aurelius, the crown of Stoicism in the second century A.D. It calculated individual worth on the basis of intellectual achievement and ethical discipline.

This brand of aristocratic individualism is mirrored in the attitudes of the Corinthian Christians. They viewed Christianity as a new philosophy and gloried in debate, competition for religious status, and in ecstatic or "spiritual" experiences. Paul sharply rebuked them because they did not properly "discern" the body of Christ (1 Cor. 11:20-22, 29). He reminded them that as a whole group they were "God's temple" (3:16). They shared a common Spirit by whom they "were all baptized into one body" (12:13). They were, he told them, "individually members of it [the body of Christ]" (12:27), and each individual's "gift" was for the "common good."

Protestantism's theological heritage of an individualistic personal gospel stems from both of these sources. In the post-Reformation theological systems of Protestant orthodoxy, the ideas and definitions of Artistotle were used as the philosophical basis and thus entered into the doctrinal formulations. At crucial points this has given orthodoxy's concept of personal salvation a rationalistic and individualistic flavor not found in the New Testament.

Orthodoxy's analysis of human nature, for example, has assumed the categories of faculty psychology which were inherited from the ancient Greeks. According to this view the individual human being is a composite of distinct, separable parts or faculties which can be dealt with as discrete units. Orthodoxy drew an especially sharp distinction between the material body and the spiritual soul as two separate parts of each person's being. The spirit or soul was conceptualized as a distinct, non-material, self-contained substance —a kind of spiritual form, containing all the human attributes in itself but living in the physical body and temporarily making use of it.

This psychological analysis, which was assumed to be the psychology of the New Testament, provided the definition and categories for orthodoxy's individualistic (not simply personalistic) view of salvation. According to this view the soul is formed independently of social interaction. (Theologians argued whether it was directly created by God or formed in the process of conception.) It reveals itself in the activity of the mind (reason) rather than in personal social relationships. Thus, salvation was a matter of the soul's relationship to God. The individual, autonomous, private soul is saved. Salvation has nothing *essentially* to do with reconciliation to fellowmen in a social experience of community. Further, it is a matter of belief—assent to correct doctrinal statements—not a matter of renewed life in community. This, as we have already seen, undercuts major biblical emphases.

Many other political, social, and scientific movements of the last century have also influenced the development of religious individualism. In order to understand the contemporary evangelical milieu, therefore, we must call attention to some of these movements.

Modern Developments

Some trace the beginning of modern self-awareness and subjectivity to the Venetians' perfection of a mirror, in which individuals could first clearly see themselves as objects. In her Scott Holland Memorial Lectures (1969), Monica Wilson explained how the growth of individual self-awareness is related to the expansion of societies themselves. Small societies that are isolated in time and space tend to be homogeneous and require identity and conformity of the individual with the group. "There is," she writes, "growth of self-awareness as men move from isolated preliterate societies to large literate societies." Extension of social contacts with different cultures through expanded travel, trade, and friendships "drive men to a greater consciousness of their own identity." Further, "as science and arts develop man's potential self-awareness increases." And as self-awareness increases, individuation, diversity, and specialization develop apace.[3]

Of course, human beings by definition are self-conscious individuals, but the degree and meaning of that individuality has apparently changed significantly in the western world within the past few centuries. Historically, tribal self-concepts equated personhood with tribal identity. Even Aristotle did not advance very far beyond this concept when he classified non-Greeks as barbarian and sub-human. To be human meant to belong to the "fatherland," that is, the homogeneous social group. Thus, for example, murder was defined as killing within the tribe; and war on neighboring tribes was not murder.

Within the recognized social unit, individuals were classified according to their sex, intelligence, emotional makeup, and social roles, and ranked from sub-human to fully human. A female, for example, had a quite different self-identity from a male; a slave from a free person; and an artisan from a noble. According to Aristotle, only a privileged few wealthy, intellectual Greek males could qualify as fully human persons and citizens of the Greek city state.

One can generalize by saying that individual self-identity was attained through solidarity with a group.[4] The question, "Who am I?" would be answered by *class*ifying oneself. Thus one might answer, "I am a laborer . . . a gentleman . . . a lady . . . a servant." Social position was a fundamental factor in self-identity, for it conditioned one's values, behavior, expectations, and even legal standing. Identity was quite an objective thing.

This kind of objective data still plays a part in individual identity, but its role is much more superficial. Today the criteria of self-awareness are more subjective. Individuals think of themselves as subjects who cannot be neatly classified on a census form.

There seems to be good historical evidence that the concept of the individual self as a highly differentiated, introspective, socially independent being came fairly late in the social development of the western world. Lionel Trilling has pointed out that the autobiography, which reflects this highly developed self-consciousness, became a fully developed literary form only as late as the seventeenth century.[5]

This new awareness of the uniqueness of the individual gave rise to an intense debate in the nineteenth and twentieth centuries about the relation of the individual to the political community. The modern debate was sparked by the French Revolution with its slogan, "Equality, Liberty and Fraternity." That revolution was not merely a rebellion of the lower classes against the upper, but a rebellion against the domination of classes over individuals, of the individual against the domination of inflexible class structures. The debate emerged as a long, intense conflict between the various ideological schools of socialism and individualism, and still is in progress.

We do not intend to review this debate in any detail, but the issues it raises have become so intertwined with western Christian theology and mission strategy that at least a summary glance seems necessary. Religious individualism in twentieth-century America cannot simply be equated with Christ-centered personalism of the apostle Paul in the first century.

As we have noted, the debate between socialism and individualism arose out of the new situation created by the French Revolution. The ideal of equalitarianism and the rise of the common citizen to a position of dignity and freedom became a dynamic force. Alongside of this political revolution, the industrial revolution was changing the economic basis of the old class structures and values. Especially in America, these forces along with the challenge of the frontier, which demanded individual courage, ingenuity, and self-sufficiency, made the strong, independent individual the great moral and spiritual ideal.

Both socialists and individualists claimed to champion the individual and the rights of the common person. Socialism developed as the argument that these new ideals of individual human fulfillment could best be achieved by completely restructuring the social order into a cooperative pattern of ownership and production. Socialists argued that true equality could come only when class distinctions and economic exploitation of the poor were overcome by the redistribution of the "means of production" (land, capital, and tools) and the reorganization of society into a cooperative community.[6] Communists, or radical socialists, who followed Karl Marx, argued that this revolution could be consistently and scientifically achieved only on the basis of a materialistic philosophy.

Individualism developed as the argument that individual fulfillment could only be achieved in a social order where each rational person was free to compete in the struggle for individual happiness. Adam Smith, who promoted this ideal of *laissez faire,* assumed however that the competitors would begin as equals. He assumed further that the free competition would keep the various interests balanced. Thus the proponents of *laissez faire* argued that individuals must be protected in their right to acquire and own wealth, and that their right of "private property" shall include the right to use it for their own profit within the limits of the law. Darwinian individualists argued this position as an application of the law of the survival of the fittest.[7]

Issues with Theological Implications

This debate raised several significant issues for religion as well as for politics. First, *what is the nature of society and the relation of the individual to it?* Individualists held that society is a kind of association formed by independent, rational individuals, who make political and social contracts with each other in their own mutual interests.[8] Socialists held that individuals have a more generic relation to society. Since they are dependent upon it, and conditioned by it, therefore they can find their individual fulfillment only within a properly organized socio-economic community.

The second issue was *the nature of human nature.* The differences here are far ranging. In fact, it was even debated whether humans have a fixed "nature." But assuming that we can in some sense speak of an essential identifiable character—and both sides did in fact assume this—what is man like? Does one have an inherent self-centered acquisitive nature which cannot be changed by historical conditioning? Or, if it can be changed at all, is it possible only over an indefinitely long period of time by an evolutionary process? Individualists answered these questions in the affirmative. Darwinian individualists held the latter view.

The socialists, with some variation, held that the nature of humans is socially and historically conditioned. They admitted that men and women in the modern western societies are in fact acquisitive, but they argued that this is because they have been formed in societies that put prime value on wealth and competition. They were confident that a "new man," a cooperative social man, could be created by changing the social environment and redirecting his values and self-image.

Third, out of the above issue arose the question of *the effectiveness and moral legitimacy of competition for wealth as the motivation for technical and cultural advancement of civilization.* The question here is whether individuals can best realize their full potential in relative independence from and in competition with their fellows, or whether individual as well as social ends are best gained by socially regulated, cooperative, or collective action.

Individualists argued that competitive labor, whether mental or physical, is the basic motivation because everyone desires his/her own happiness. Thus freedom means, among other things, the right to individual "pursuit of happiness." In the Declaration of Independence, for example, Jefferson wrote that men are "endowed by their Creator" with this "inalienable right." The covert assumption is that through competitive action, *enlightened self-interest* will in the long run achieve the highest good. Reason will prevail.

Socialists held that unrestrained competition for wealth leads to exploitation of the weak and the inequitable distribution of the earth's material resources. They were persuaded that collective action provides a more rational and effective approach to the production and fair distribution of wealth and individual opportunity. Convinced that human drives and motivations are the product of social conditioning, they called for the revolutionary reorganization of society along socialist lines in order to begin the process of change in human nature itself.

All these issues came to an explosive focus in the issue of private property. Can the individual's right to accumulate and use private property for his/her own advantage be morally justified? What role does private property play in social and economic development? Is it, as the radical socialists claimed, the root of mankind's troubles? Or is it the legitimate, "sacred" extension of individual selfhood as the individualists argued?

The Impact of Individualism

Historically, the alliance of American evangelicalism with individualism is quite understandable. For one thing, most proponents of socialism were forthrightly anti-church, and some, like Karl Marx, were explicitly naturalistic and materialistic in their assumptions. Socialism arose at a time when orthodox Christian institutions were very closely allied to the upper economic classes. Thus, in the struggle to overcome classism, many socialists viewed the church as an enemy. I point this out as an historical coincidence because in fact some of their social concepts were not essentially contrary to the teaching of the Bible.

Although Marx championed the "real" individual and the "whole" person, he clearly reduced the definition of reality to material-social dimensions; and in rejecting the human spiritual dimension he inevitably destroyed the basis for the individual's transcending value. If the individual person is merely a material historical unit in the socio-economic collective, there is no reason to attribute to him/her more than unitary value. Therefore the collective must be viewed as logically prior to and of greater value than the individual.[9] One is not surprised, then, that in spite of the high-sounding humanist goals of Communist socialism, the individual has often been treated as a highly expendable means to the ends of society.

On the other hand, in America the ideals of rational individualism exalted the dignity and rights of the individual, political self-determination, and moral responsibility.[10] The struggle for a "free" church based upon individual Christian experience and a voluntary church covenant was intimately associated with the emergence of a new society of free men governed under a self-imposed political contract. And both of these ideal social goals were firmly based upon faith in the rational, morally self-determining individual working for his own enlightened self-interest. "Enlightened self-interest was a means to an end which was not self-interest but a free society."[11] As one author put it in the *Boston Quarterly Review* (1841):

> Individualism has its immutable laws . . . which . . . when allowed to operate without let or hindrance,—however at first . . . their effects may appear destructive and anarchical,—must, in the end, assimilate the species, and evolve all the glorious phenomena of original and eternal *order;*—that order which exists in man himself, and alone vivifies and sustains him.[12]

The Evangelical Synthesis

Philosophically, rational individualism provided the base for both liberal and conservative theology. The new

ideas and assumptions were absorbed, and the new definitions were discreetly used to enhance the evangelical cause
as well as that of liberalism. In this respect their systems are
more similar than they are different. However, no significant
social theology developed within conservative Protestantism
to match the social gospel within the liberal camp.

Ostensibly the case for evangelical individualism is
based upon the Bible, and in popular guise it is often equated
with the Christ-centered personalism of the apostle Paul. To
be more exact, it is based theologically on a scholastic interpretation of biblical texts inherited in large part from
seventeenth-century Protestant orthodoxy. Aristotelian definitions of human nature have been significant in its formation, but the breath of a new age has enlivened the body of
this revived Aristotelian-biblical syntheses. Its cogency and
impact owes fully as much to the new political and moral
self-awareness of individuals as to the emotional fervor of
revivalism or the spiritual power of Scripture.

We need to analyze the elements of this synthesis carefully if we are to evaluate the theological implications and the
socio-political associations of evangelicalism. What rightly
claims to be biblical, and what is of extra-biblical vintage,
both ancient and modern?

To begin with, Aristotle's concept of the rational soul as
the distinctly human faculty was equated with the biblical
idea of "the image of God" *in* man. (Note that whereas the
Bible speaks of the whole *adam* created in God's image, this
theological construct thinks of the image as a particular
aspect or faculty *in man's composite being.*) The interpretation of the creation account assumed that *"adam"* meant
individual man. Indeed, in the first instance it was understood to mean the male sex. Thus, according to this theological interpretation, God has breathed into each person an
immortal rational soul which endows him/her with infinite
worth.

The essential human quality, which we refer to as personal, inheres in the rational soul, which is a non-material
substance formed by a creative act of God *apart from social
intercourse.* "Personhood" is a discretely individual category,

105

perceived as both non-material and non-social in its essence. Thus the concept of an autonomous individual person logically prior to the social group and, by implication, completely personal without a community of discourse, was established as a theological presupposition.

The various communities in society, such as nation and church, were perceived as collectives of individuals based upon legal and social contracts. This, as we have seen in the last chapter, is inadequate to communicate the full biblical meaning of person as individual-in-community. Indeed, it is far more faithful to Aristotle via John Locke and J. S. Mill than to the Hebrew-Christian tradition.

It follows that since the soul is the essential component of the human being, salvation essentially involves only the soul or spirit. In tripartite systems of analysis, the spirit is primarily involved, and then the soul and body in an inferential and indefinite chain of results. The crux is a "spiritual" conversion which assures salvation from an equally "spiritual" or "theological" judgment. Its social dimensions are quite non-essential.

This salvation is guaranteed by God's election of the individual. His covenant of grace is made with each individual in a private transaction apart from any behavioral or social conditions. As a result of revivalism, the emphasis changed over the years from God's election to the Christian's experience of salvation, but the focus remained upon the individual. Philip Schaff put it succinctly in the 1840s when he wrote that the divine mission of Protestantism was "to place each individual soul in immediate union with Christ and his Word; to complete in each one the work of redemption; to build in each one a temple of God, a spiritual church; and to unfold and sanctify all the energies of the individual."[13]

Conversion, according to evangelical individualism, is a change within the soul (the rational faculty) which is reflected primarily in a rational change of belief patterns called faith. It does not effect an essential change in individuals' social nature. They remain self-centered and acquisitive, or, in theological language, *fallen*. Of course, change in the soul/spirit is expected to influence social behavior and relationships. Saved individuals will, or should, be more loving, honest, and altruistic, but conversion does not change the fundamental patterns of individual-group relations. Again, in theological terms salvation, strictly speaking, does not intrinsically include reconciliation with one's fellowmen. Hopefully such reconciliation will follow as a result of salvation.

Thus, in effect the evangelical Protestant position agrees with the individualist view that historical, individual human nature is an unchangeable given. It stands adamantly opposed to the socialist contention that human nature is socially conditioned, and has identified this belief as the fatal flaw in the Social Gospel. It has insisted that the human soul, not human nature, is transformed by a supernatural conversion. Any talk of community and social conditioning is considered to be implicitly, if not explicitly, naturalistic. Until we comprehend this basic postulate, we shall never understand the adamant bias of evangelical theology against any definition of person as a social reality or of salvation as a social process.

Since conversion does not change human nature fundamentally, competition and the rule of law remain the normative regulating principles, not only for the social order but for Christians in the social order. The nature of the group relation, process, and control mechanism remains essentially unchanged because mankind in their social-historical dimensions remain essentially unchanged. We may expect in the church a new degree of cooperation and mutual caring; and we may hope that the saved individuals will compete fairly and with at least a modicum of compassion in the worldly order. But by theological definition, salvation does not introduce us to a fundamentally new order of relationships in which the private principal is superseded by commonality as the basic operational assumption. Private gain, even in the religious sphere, remains the primary motivator. Hence the strong insistence on "the *sacred right* of private property."

The question is whether this insistence upon the social

autonomy of the individual is logically necessary to a consistent belief in God's supernatural intervention for mankind's salvation. Must the biblical materials be interpreted in individualistic categories in order to do justice to their message of salvation for the individual person? It obviously has been the implied contention of this essay that it is not. If I may paraphrase Galatians 6:16, I have argued that "individualism is nothing; socialism is nothing; the only thing that counts is a new creation." And that new creation is the new individual-in-community.

Following the political model of Locke and Rousseau, evangelical Protestantism, both conservative and liberal, has understood the church as an association of believers who join together for their mutual religious purposes such as worship, nurture, and mission.

Elect individuals who have received assurance of salvation through proper experiential signs[14] contract in voluntary covenant to form a church. Thus the free congregation of individual believers in contractual association for mutually agreed upon purposes has become the unquestioned model for authentic Christian community. In fact, the only organic communal basis for the congregation was the family unit. Clearly, then, the church is not considered essential to the salvation of the individual but only instrumental.[15] The precedence of the individual and his/her religious autonomy are firmly established by a clear, logical, theological rationale.

Evaluating the Effects

Evangelical Protestantism's greatest strength has been its cultivation of a dynamic, satisfying, personal faith which gives motivation, guidance, and strength to the individual. It has cultivated an immediate relationship with God, a personal sense of his presence and guidance, a strong reliance upon his power, and a comforting submission to his will in all things. It has waged a vigorous campaign to bring individuals to decision for Christ, and has inspired them to win others in personal evangelism. In fact the evangelizing of those completely outside the Christian churches, both at home and abroad, has been largely the work of evangelicals. Spreading Bible knowledge has been accented as a major goal of the movement. It has inculcated a deep personal piety and moral conscience. The man and woman of God, clear-eyed, smiling, and confident with a Bible in one hand and the other reached out to receive penitent sinners, has been its trademark.

By virtue of historical circumstances, American evangelicalism has been activistic, gregarious, and democratic. But it has also had its serious weaknesses. The effects of religious individualism have not all been good. Indeed, as so often is the case, its strengths have become its most seductive temptations!

The most conspicuous weakness of evangelical Protestant theology has been *its lack of understanding and witness to authentic community as the fulfillment of the believer's personal relation to God.* Its intuitive, operational conception of the private individual as the essentially personal unit has indisposed it for organic community beyond the nuclear family. Its corporate trademark is the voluntary occasional fellowship and the incorporated association. That the climax of personal spiritual fulfillment is a social experience of God rather than a private mystical one simply does not fit the categories of individualism. In fact, in common evangelical language, "social" has become an antonym of "personal." Thus one often hears "social gospel" contrasted to "personal gospel."

Individualistic religion has tended to degrade the social experience of spiritual reality as legalism and formalism. The social and behavioral expressions of religious conviction have been relegated to the theological category of "works," and have been suspect as a facade for humanism—as though there were something inherently more humanistic about the social expression of religion than its psychological expression!

When the social dimensions of personal religious experience are negated, compensation is made by accenting the psychological aspects. Subjective criteria become the norm for reality and truth in religious profession. Spirituality is defined in terms of personality characteristics, belief patterns, and personal piety. Words, feelings, and attitudes take precedence over action and steadfast relationships. For example, love tends to become a theological virtue and sympathetic feeling, rather than a deed and moral relationship. The personal, religious quality of social intercourse is judged in terms of emotional intensity and spontaneity, and the model for religious fellowship *(koinonia)* tends to become sporadic intimacy—the occasional spiritual high or "revival," rather than a dependable structured relationship of responsible caring.

This bias has weakened the authenticity of evangelicalism's witness to the gospel. Fortunately, however, its performance has often been better than its theoretical understandings because its adherents are genuine persons who transcend their own rational constructs.

Individualism has also had a marked effect on the content and style of normative Protestant *religious experience*. By definition, the personal experience with God is essentially a private (non-social) and rational communication, independent of the community of God's people. And a God who is privately and independently accessible easily turns into a private God—one who belongs to me! He responds to me (first). He blesses my luxury even in the face of others' poverty. He saves me, my family, and nation, even at the expense of others. He protects my private property which he has given me the right to claim. He furthers my causes which, of course, I have planned for his kingdom. At any rate, our prayers often go this way. A private two-way relation with god—yes, a small *g* because he has become an idol.

Privacy in this case does not mean the aloneness of the prayer closet. It means independence of, and what Samuel Miller once called "shut-up-ness" from, our fellows.[16] Neither are we suggesting something less than an intimate personal relationship in prayer. The question is whether prayer and our relationship to God is a "private affair," that is, exclusive of the community of faith. Individualistic religion has failed to appreciate the real significance of the plural pronouns in *"Our* Father," and "Give *us* this day *our* daily bread."[17]

Religious individualism, then, has tended to make the satisfaction of individual needs and desires the goal of religion. I go to "the church of my choice." I worship for the inspiration and renewed strength I receive, and I pray in order to receive God's blessings rather than to bless God. It is common to hear the complaint that a particular congregation or pastor "does not meet my needs," as though that were the final criterion. Self-fulfillment and the good life, whether explicit or disguised as "victory in Christ," are considered the legitimate primary end of religious profession and practice.

Individualism has also had its impact on evangelical strategy in both organization and witness. In evangelism the lone individual has been the target. Everything focuses upon a private decision and the genuineness of interior change. The evangelistic message is highly specialized in content and purpose, whether communicated one-to-one or in mass.

This has inevitably led to a preoccupation with the number of decisions for Christ, as can easily be documented in the history of revivalism from Charles G. Finney in the 1830s to Wilbur Chapman and Billy Sunday in the early 1900s.

At a recent mass evangelistic rally, where tens of thousands were gathered for inspiration and instruction in evangelistic techniques, a teenager gleefully testified to the mass audience that she had saved nineteen individuals in one hour that very afternoon. Her testimony was greeted with cheers, and the leaders of the rally, who were nationally known, professional evangelists, gave her unqualified praise! Without disparaging the sincerity of either the soul winner or her converts, we can point out the obvious lack of social or community dimensions in such evangelistic operations.

Mass evangelism techniques have proved most popular in spreading individualistic religion. The mass rally is the individualist's surrogate for authentic community. The individual, taken from his/her accustomed social setting, finds instant camaraderie and emotional support to make a decision. At the same time, the crowd of strangers provides the anonymity and impersonal context for decision-making which perforce turns it into a "private" commitment, with a minimum of continuing accountability to a community of God's people. The acknowledged weak point of this technique has been its difficulty in relating converts to local congregations. What has not been so clearly recognized is that the mass-meeting technique, even when it is an interchurch cooperative effort, models a concept of "salvation" and creates a spiritual climate that militate against genuine community.

Evangelical missionary strategy outside of "Christendom" has followed the same individualistic assumptions and tactics. The message of God's gracious rule in Christ has been communicated solely as a call for individuals to religious conversion. Individualistic strategy did not call for planting the Word as a seed in the soil of other cultural communities. It has in fact viewed all cultures outside Christendom as antithetical to the message of Christ, and on principle it has insisted that individuals separate from their "non-Christian" society and culture in order to save their souls.[18] Nor can it be said that such strategy has created authentic communities to replace the personal-social realities which the convert has given up. Many years ago Charles Andrews, the famous British missionary to India, noted that Moslems who were deeply impressed by Christ were nevertheless hesitating to leave their Muslim communities because they had no Christian community alternative.

Biblical Personalism—an Alternative

To be a person in the biblical sense is to be a subject, an "I," in relation with another subject, a "thou," under the covenant of God. A person is an *indiviual-in-community*. Not only is such a person a mind-body (psycho-somatic) unity, but also a social-spiritual unity. Outside of authentic relationships in community, personhood is a mere capacity. Mature personhood is the gift of God in covenant community. In New Testament language we speak of it as wholeness or maturity in Christ.[19] And very obviously the biblical concept of salvation is closely associated with such mature personhood.

One needs only to reflect momentarily to realize how fundamental the community of salvation is to the individual. We come to the knowledge of God through the ongoing community. That some isolated individuals have found Christ through a chance reading of Scripture apart from knowledge of the community is the exception that proves the rule! Even in such cases, had there been no community of witness, there would have been no translated Scripture to have been read.[20]

Our experience of God is profoundly conditioned by the community. Our continuing relation to him is sustained and nurtured in community. Our religious convictions are expressed in our social responses—caring, sharing, forgiving, and receiving forgiveness. Spirituality and holiness are not ontological attributes or subjective psychological attitudes, but objective social relationships and consistent actions in communion with God and our fellows.

Thus, personal religious experience must be understood as both social and individual, but never as private. We come as individual persons to God, but our relationship to him can never be exclusive of the brother. Authentic prayer, in which that relationship is expressed, is never "I" centered. It is kingdom centered, always made in the context of the community and its purposes. Every prayer must be addressed to *"our* Father," that is, it must be prayed in an attitude of openness to the brother and sister for their good as well as my own. We must always pray as individuals-in-community. To pray "in the name of Christ" is to pray as one who recognizes Christ as head of the body and oneself as a functioning member under his headship.

Notes to Chapter IV

1. In this chapter I have not attempted to make a full analysis and comparison of the whole spectrum of conservative and liberal thought in Protestantism. I am concerned rather with that broad central position which may be called evangelical. Within

the broad center of the theological continuum, the evangelical liberal and his more traditional counterpart in fact have much in common. It is extremely difficult to associate this position exclusively with one denomination, seminary, or ecumenical organization, but it seems to be increasingly represented in that fluid amalgam of conservative Protestantism which calls itself evangelical, in contrast to fundamentalists. Even within the last decade these lines have been shifting and broadening significantly.

2. See Ernst Troeltsch, *Protestantism and Progress*, Putnam's Sons, 1912: "But modern Individualism is not primarily based on the Renaissance. It is based, rather, on the idea, which is essentially Christian, of the destination of man to acquire perfected personality through the ascent to God as the source both of all personal life and also of the world.... This spiritual temper was founded by Christianity and the Israelitish prophetism" (p. 34).

3. Monica Wilson, *Religion and the Transformation of Society*, Cambridge University Press, 1971. See chapter 1, especially pp. 14–23.

4. In modern Japan, which on the surface appears to be a secular, western-type technocracy, subtle but pervasive differences still exist. The structure of group relationships, self-images, motivation patterns, and therefore moral valuations and responses, all bear witness to a different concept of the individual and his place in the group.

   Self-identity *(jibun)* is a possession which is received through participation in the group—traditionally the extended family, clan, and nation. It is achieved through a delicate balance of individual self-assertion and submission. But, in any case, it is quite impossible to "have a self" apart from strong and intimate relations of dependency and responsibility to the group. To be isolated from the group is to lose one's self. See Takeo Doi, *The Anatomy of Dependence*, Kodansha International Ltd., 1973, pp. 132ff.

5. Lionel Trilling, *Sincerity and Authenticity*, Harvard University Press, 1972, pp. 19ff.

6. See Adam Schaff, *Marxism and the Human Individual*, McGraw-Hill, 1970; and Guido De Ruggiero, *The History of European Liberalism*, Beacon, 1959 (paperback), 1927 (first edition), pp. 381–94, for historical background.

7. See Richard Hofstadter, *Social Darwinism in American Thought*, Beacon Press, 1955.

8. The political philosophy underlying this position was spelled

out by John Locke (1632–1704) and Jacques Rousseau (1712–1778). J. S. Mill (1806–1873) carried the idea of individual liberty and non-interference of government even further. He spoke of society as a collective of "the separate individuals who compose it," and held that each individual has an absolute right to "self-government," with the one exception that their behavior should not harm others. See the introductory chapter of his essay "On Liberty."

In his "Remarks on Associations," William Ellery Channing wrote, "Society is chiefly important as it ministers to and calls forth intellectual and moral energy and freedom [of the individual]. . . . According to these views, our social nature and connections are means. Inward power is the end,—a power which is to triumph over and control the influence of society." *Channing's Works*, Boston, 1882, p. 140.

For excellent examples of the way in which the case for exclusive individual ownership of property and competition for profit were argued from a theology based on the Scottish "Common Sense Philosophy," see Joseph Dorfman, *Thorstein Veblen and His America*, Viking, 1945 (4th printing), pp. 19ff.

9. Interestingly enough, what individualism and socialism had in common was their assumed definition of the social group as a collective. When the relation of the individual and the group is conceived as the single unit to the collective, the psychological tension between individual and group turns into a logical contradiction, especially for individualism. The individual as a discrete unit is endowed with "infinite worth," and the group is viewed as a collective of infinitely valuable ends in themselves. Where there is conflict of interests, one "infinite" is opposed to the other.

Marx intended to resolve this contradiction in the synthesis of the classless society, but when he reduced all reality to the material and defined the "real" individual as the historical-physical personality, he inevitably and radically subjected the individual to the group. He destroyed the grounds for transcendence of the individual. The group became his sole point of reference for self-identity and criterion for meaning.

10. Yehoshua Arieli, *Individualism and Nationalism in American Ideology*, Harvard University Press, 1964: "The term [individualism], which in the Old World was almost synonymous with selfishness, social anarchy, and individual self-assertion, connoted in America self-determination, moral freedom, the rule of liberty, and the dignity of man." P. 193.

11. *Ibid.*, p. 198.

12. *Ibid.*, p. 199.

13. Philip Schaff, *America, A Sketch of its Political, Social, and Religious Character*, ed. by Perry Miller, Belknap Press, 1961, p. 101.

14. Jonathan Edwards in *A Treatise Concerning Religious Affections* (1746) attempted to analyze and determine the valid from the counterfeit experience. Sydney Ahlstrom has commented that in New England Puritanism, "for the first time in centuries (if not ever) the conversion experience was made normative for church membership on a wide and comprehensive scale." See "Theology in America: A Historical Survey" in Smith and Jamison, *The Shaping of American Religion*, Vol. I, Princeton University Press, 1961, p. 240.

15. In this regard it takes its precedent from and is faithful to John Calvin.

16. See Samuel H. Miller, *The Great Realities*, Harper, 1955, pp. 95ff.

17. Paul Verghese (Bishop Mar Gregorius) notes, "Prayer goes astray when it is ultimately focused on gaining immediate ends for ourselves—however noble and 'spiritual' those ends may be." *The Joy of Freedom*, John Knox Press, 1967, p. 83.

18. The "Church Growth" strategy, which has been accepted by many evangelicals in recent years, has challenged this older strategy. But it must be noted that the movement did not grow out of evangelical presuppositions, nor is it entirely consistent with current evangelical theology in that it plays down the significance of individual conversion as the starting point for church building.

19. I have no intention of denying that there is a *subject* (person or soul) which lies back of and is the center of unity for the personality. But that subject is a malleable, growing essence, not a static one. And it is this subject or person that Christian faith identifies with the spirit which will be given an immortal form in the final resurrection (1 Cor. 15:51–54). It is the person that gives continuity to life here and beyond death.

    Psychologists are extremely leery of speaking of the person as an essence or soul. Many will only use personality, ego-center, or similar terms. Peter Bertocci, who has struggled with this problem as a Christian scholar, offers the following definition for ethical purposes: "Thus we may define the person, for ethical purposes, as a complex, self-identifying continuant unity whose activities involve psychic and physiological events." Bertocci and Millard, *Personality and the Good*, McKay, 1963, p. 154.

20. Protestant orthodoxy set up the inerrant Scriptures as the historical nexus for the rational soul's knowledge of God. But while Scripture may be the logical nexus, we must remember that Scripture does not exist apart from the existence of a people of God. And for each of us, the religious community has brought Scripture to us, or us to Scripture, as the case may be. Someone has observed that the song, "Jesus loves me, this I know/ for the *Bible* tells me so," might more accurately read "Jesus loves me, this I know/ for my *mother* tells me so."

V

HALLMARKS OF AUTHENTIC COMMUNITY

Authentic community is community according to the original intention of creation. In the Christian faith we believe that the pattern of that authenticity is seen most clearly in Jesus. However, the authentic community did not begin historically in the period A.D. 28–30. The biblical theme of community begins with creation.

In this chapter we examine the nature of that community as the community of witness. What are its marks of authenticity? How can we recognize the visible church in mission? We have already noted that we cannot simply identify it with organized religious institutions. What is its essential theological nature?

Chapters Seven and Eight deal more directly with the question of how the church carries out the mission of Christ in the world.

A Biblical Overview

God made mankind to live in a social community under a covenant which he gave to them. Aristotle spoke of man as a "rational animal," and Christian theology borrowed that definition from him. But the Bible speaks of man as the *covenant* animal. *Adam* (both male and female, Gen. 1:27; 5:2) was made to live in covenant community. Human self-realization or personhood is found in responsible confrontation and interaction with other persons, and ultimately in confrontation with God in the acceptance of responsibility under the covenant.

The Bible refers to this capacity of mankind for personal relationship to God, and therefore to each other, as the "image of God" in mankind. Thus, God's image implies authentic community, but that image was marred "in *Adam*." It has been fully revealed only in Christ. So Christ, and not *Adam*, is the authentic man, and the pattern of authentic community is to be seen in him. Jesus Christ came to renew the covenant between God and mankind which was broken already at the source of human history—"in *Adam*." We must, however, speak of it as more than a renewal, for what was realized in Christ was far more than any prior covenant had achieved. Through him a new kind of covenant and the "new creation" of community were accomplished (Gal. 6:15; 2 Cor. 5:17).

The new order in Christ is therefore genetically related to the community implied in the original creation. The same "Word" by whom all things were created came into that world, and from within recreated a new humanity or "race,"[1] and with it the possibility for authentic community. That possibility for community is not a substitute for the original community of creation, but the fulfillment of it. In the "second creation," as Bonhoeffer noted, "part of the world is made afresh after the image of God (Col. 3:10); . . . A part of the world has been made anew. That is the founding of the church."[2] The church, as the New Testament speaks of it, is the recreation of the human possibility for community which was implied in creation and realized first in Christ. It has become possible for us through his resurrection and the coming of the Holy Spirit.

In order to make this first point as an introduction to what follows, we have omitted discussion of mankind's sin, which, of course, is the reason why a "new creation" or "recreation" is needed. We will return to that in a moment, but here let me underscore the significance of the biblical idea that authentic community has its origin in both the first creation and the "new creation." This means that the church is in the mainstream of God's intention for human well-being, as envisioned in creation. It is not a sacramental reality in contrast to the real reality of the socio-political world, as one church leader inadvertently put it. Neither is it experienced as a mystical, inner reality or spiritual fellowship in contrast to the web of social relationships that make up the reality of our personal existence. The existence of the church as authentic community signals the new possibility for transforming those relationships through "nonconformity" to the old order and "renewal" of our minds (Rom. 12:1–2). This possibility gives our proposed discussion its crucial and exciting importance.

Defining Community

Communities may be groups, but not all groups are communities. Statistical groups such as all males under twenty-five, for example, are not a community although they have something in common. An audience in a lecture hall is not a community even though it has met for a common experience. Even students in a class that meets over a span of time are not necessarily a community. While a society such as a corporation or association formed to accomplish some limited objective of the group may develop community relationships, it need not be and often is not a community. *A community is defined by the special quality of relationships which are formed in it.*

It has also been amply demonstrated in our urban society that physical or geographical proximity of a group does not necessarily mean community. Many giant apartment buildings with hundreds of families living in smothering proximity utterly lack the spirit of community, and in many urban "neighborhoods" the residents come and go with almost no mutual recognition! Some of the ingredients of community are mutual acceptance, and the responsibility for each other implied by that acceptance, interdependence, participation in group decision-making, and identity through involvement with the group.

In community the *person,* not the individual, is the elemental unit. To use the jargon of Martin Buber, the "I-Thou" relationship is at the heart of community.[3] A person is an individual in such an I-Thou relationship, that is, not an independent and isolated individual. Community is not a collection of individuals, but a fellowship of persons. In community interdependence and involvement exist; this enhances individual personhood and provides personal identity.

Because the word community is used in so many different ways and in the context of so many varied ideologies, we need also to explain that a community, as we are using the word, does not mean a collective. A collective farm, for example, is not necessarily a community. In a collective, whether it be a socialistic association or capitalistic corporation, the individual may remain private and even isolated from relationships that foster personal identity and growth. Further, in such collectives the individual particularities are suppressed in favor of the collective group and its objectives. Indeed, this may be one reason why collectivization as a political method in socialism has not been particularly effective in producing community.

Community, then, is *a group of people who have formed a pattern of interdependent and reciprocal relationships which aim at enhancing the personal quality of the group itself.*[4] What people in community have in common is each other and the mutual enhancement of each person in their life together.

Luke described the first Christian community at Jerusalem as a group who were of "one heart and life (psyche)." The community also has outside objectives, as we shall see, but it is this reciprocal affirmation of each other as persons in Christ, and acceptance of mutual responsibility, which is implied in such an affirmation that defines the Christian community. A second definitive characteristic of the Christian community is that its objective for the world outside its immediate perimeter is the same as for itself. It is, in Bonhoeffer's pregnant phrase, "for the world." It calls the world to the new possibility of peace *(shalom)* in Christ.

The World as Broken Community

Mankind was created to find wholeness and personal fulfillment in community under God. Sin destroyed that original possibility. Mankind broke the covenant which provided for their well-being (*shalom*) in community with God and fellow man. Their rejection of God's covenant is described as disobedience in eating from the "tree of the knowledge of good and evil." It is called the "tree of the knowledge of good and evil" because its fruit was the occasion for the original moral decision, but what was the nature of that choice? As many commentators have pointed out, the "knowledge of good and evil" does not indicate primarily an awareness of the difference between right and wrong. Rather, it means the knowledge of how to achieve the good things in life and avoid the evils. The tree and its fruit represent the possibility of power for achievement and self-agrandizement through knowledge. The grasping for that power in the face of their creator's prohibition was their original sin.

From this perspective we can begin to understand the true character of sin and its consequences. *Adam's* temptation was to choose for self ahead of God and neighbor—"me first!" Sin entered as an act of primal selfishness in which the individual asserted his/her private right to the fruits of knowledge and power in the face of and at the expense of God and fellow humans. Thus, sin was a denial and rejection of the original community. The curse on sin followed as an intrinsic consequence. It affected the most elemental social and ecological relationships which are the very foundations of community (Gen. 3:16–19).

The consequences of Adam and Eve's sin are immediately evident in their first child, Cain (Gen. 4:1–16). Cain viewed his brother as a threat and enemy to his own well-being and therefore killed him. He denied his responsibility in community, and because of his sin he became a "fugitive and wanderer on the earth."

In an attempt to remedy the curse, Cain settled in Nod and began to build a city. Thus originated the *city of man*— the human community built on technical civilization and human prowess. And according to the terse and highly suggestive story that follows (vv. 17ff.), Cain's descendents are the purveyors of a "civilization" characterized by polygamy and violence.

The story, different yet always the same, is told again in Genesis 11. Mankind, in their pretentious pride, build their idolatrous community with a "tower to heaven." The tower is most likely a symbol of the mythical sacred axis and marks the center of the earth. Around that sacred "center," *which they have determined and built*, they expect to find security and achievement of the good life. They plan to form a power bloc and control their fate through their own skill. The curse, which again follows as intrinsic consequence, is the confusion of language (the *sine qua non* of community), and they are scattered over the face of the earth to become the warring tribes and nations of the ancient world.

This frustrating story of high hopes and disappointing consequences continues to the present. The promise of knowledge ends in disillusionment. The shortcuts of violent power shatter the same community they are intended to build and protect. The world of secular promise—of technical achievement and cultural accomplishment—is experienced as *broken community*.

But this is only part of the story. Alongside the community of man symbolized in Cain's city and Babel is another community. Its origin is with Seth, and in it are found Enoch, "who walked with God," and Noah, of whom it was prophesied, "this one shall bring us relief" from the Lord's curse upon the earth (Gen. 5:29). This community also lived under the continuing judgment of death, and it was constantly vulnerable to apostasy (Gen: 6:1–6) through alliances and compromise with the civilization of Cain and his descendents. Such alliances appeared to be advantageous. According to the account, the "daughters of men" were highly desirable and the children of the unions were "giants." But the end was the multiplication of perversion and evil. Even so, the fragmented reality of the original community was preserved by God through Noah's family when he was faithful to the covenant.

The story of this fragmentation of the original community, which becomes the dominant theme of the rest of the Bible, is picked up again with Abraham. He too, like Cain, was a nomad, but with a difference. He was called to leave Ur of the Chaldees (the city of man) in quest of the city of God (Heb. 11:10). He lived as a "stranger and pilgrim" in the desert, faithful to the covenant which held the promise of authentic community. He understood that community can not be built by human prowess, but that it is given now only in token (birth of Isaac) and in promise of future fulfillment (Gen. 12:1–3). Thus his nomadic community, wandering among the settled tribes and cities of his day, became a sign—an authentic witness to the original community.

It is not our purpose to follow the story further. The analysis of the human situation so deftly portrayed in the stories of the early chapters of Genesis is completed with the story of Abraham. This analysis supplies the preface to the formation of Israel (the "children of Abraham") as the "people" or community of God. In summary it runs something like this: The intention of God in creation was thwarted by disobedience. Having rejected God's covenant of life and peace, mankind attempted to build a surrogate community based on self-interest and violence. But God continued to call mankind to authentic community both through judgment on their substitute community and through the continued offer of a covenant relationship.

Metanoia—the Renewed Possibility

In our world of broken covenants, the original community can be known only as the community of repentance. Indeed, repentance, or *metanoia,* is the hallmark of authentic community.

This was a key insight of the Protestant reformers, and has remained a primary doctrine in orthodox Protestant circles. Unfortunately, however, through the centuries its meaning has eroded until it is practically equated with regret for past misdeeds, contrition, and confession which are the human grounds for forgiveness. This usage is clearly reflected in the English language dictionaries which equate it with *penitence*. The New Testament meaning goes much beyond this. To say "community of repentance" means more than community of those confessing their daily sins ("doing pennance") or community of forgiven sinners who continue to acknowledge that they are sinners (penitents).

In order to indicate the fuller dimensions of the meaning of repentance, I will use the original New Testament word *metanoia* (pronounced *mét-e-nóy-a*). The noun *metanoia* literally means a change of mind or a reorientation of perception and understanding. In verb form it is related to the word *epistrephō*, which means to turn around or convert; and it overlaps in meaning with the synonym *metamellomai*, which means to have a change in feelings—regret or remorse. The primary emphasis in *metanoia*, however, is on reorientation of life—what the Bible calls our "walk," and what we today refer to as life-style.[5]

Metanoia is a radical (going to the roots) change of mind and heart which results in a revolutionary reorientation of both individual life-style and social patterns. One changes fundamentally from autonomy and self-sufficiency to community under the covenant. This new stance is beautifully displayed in the life of the first community at Jerusalem, which recognized Jesus as the Christ. Acts 4:32 says of them that "they were of one heart and soul; and no one said of his possessions, 'It is my exclusive property,' but they held them to be common property for mutual benefit."

Metanoia is first a reorientation toward God, who is the source and ultimate meaning of life. Of course, there is for us an element of penitence—self-reproach and regret—in our repentance, because as we turn toward God we see more clearly how offensive and hurtful our old self-assertiveness has been. But "repentance from dead works and faith toward God" (Heb. 6:1) is primarily a decisive shift in attitude or stance and only incidentally feelings of regret and guilt.

Jesus' attitude toward God is our model of the repentant stance, as Matthew's account of his baptism and temptation certainly implies. As the "pioneer and perfecter of our faith" (Heb. 12:2) he submitted to the baptism of repentance by

John the Baptist. Matthew, conscious of the possible implications of this act, notes that Jesus was baptized in order to "fulfill all righteousness." His repentance was not a matter of penitence or regret, but of the "righteousness of God," that is, he was demonstrating the true righteousness which God requires.[6] In this act of "repentance" Jesus publicly took the position of a son and servant in relation to God. As he stood thus before God in the attitude of repentance, the voice from heaven declared him to be in truth the "beloved Son."

The new character of repentance is portrayed in the temptation story which follows immediately upon the baptism. In each approach Satan tempted Jesus, the Son, to revert to the way of *Adam* and old Israel, both of whom are also referred to as God's sons. Each time Jesus refused the temptations. He declared his absolute dependence upon God, and his acceptance of his life and mission as God's gift.

In the first temptation Satan urged Jesus to assert himself and to use his power as "Son of God" to make a name for himself in the world. Jesus was tempted to be ambitious and use his power for his own advantage—in this case to feed himself. Note how this directly parallels the temptation of the first *Adam* to gain knowledge and power for his own good.

In the second approach Satan suggested that perhaps the "God" by whose words Jesus has pledged to live is not really present and available. He was alluding to the experience of Israel at Massah when they put the Lord to the test and demanded a demonstration to prove whether "the Lord is among us or not" (Ex. 16:7; Deut. 6:16).

In the last assault Jesus was tempted to be "realistic" by compromising with the power that actually rules the world. It was implied that he did not need to completely reject God, but only to be pragmatic in his approach to the real locus of power in this world. Here the question of how the authentic community is to be formed is bluntly stated.

In each response Jesus decisively turned from the suggestion of the adversary, and declared his allegiance and submission to the covenant. As the one who is to call forth the new Israel, he pledged *full obedience* to all the words of

God. When, like Israel of old, he was led through the "humiliation" of hunger and insecurity in the wilderness (Deut. 8:3), he refused to demand proof, maintaining complete trust. And at the risk of complete failure and loss of life, he gave *undivided loyalty* to the only Lord, God. These are the hallmarks of a repentant life.

Metanoia expresses itself as a reorientation of the whole personality in relationships with others. The demand for independence, which at best requires toleration of others, is exchanged for a willing admission of interdependence which gladly assumes mutual responsibilities as a matter of justice. Indeed, it goes beyond reciprocal justice and acts unilaterally for the good of the other. Aggressive self-assertion and the manipulative use of power for one's own private advantage are repudiated for a "gentle spirit" (Matt. 5:5). The classical term for this gentle spirit is meekness, which, I might interject, has nothing in common with passivity, excessive inhibition, or mousiness! Meekness is that grace of accepting what comes to us in life, and thus freeing us from pushiness—the aggressiveness which grows out of resentment and envy.[7]

Metanoia is conversion from the closed posture of self-defense and self-justification to the openness of affirmation and honest confession. It opens us to others, making it possible for us to genuinely identify with their concerns and joys. Thus others' *needs* are recognized as their *rights,* rather than our burdens to be endured. This openness is the spirit of *koinonia. Metanoia* is the dynamic of *shalom,* that peace of God which is the well-being of true community.

That such a reorientation of individual attitudes is fundamental to community seems so obvious that it may come as something of a surprise when we note that systems of the world utterly ignore it in their prescriptions for national and world unity. Political systems substitute the balance of power and the enactment of effective laws.[8] The judicial process acknowledges its desirability, but has no legal way to recognize and deal with it. Education systems continue to place their faith in the acquisition of knowledge and the dynamics of technology. Humanitarian social work ignores it, and places its hopes on education. Industry and business not only ignore it, they virtually repudiate it in favor of competition and efficiency as the ingredients of success. Even institutionalized religion has by and large reduced it to a liturgical confession that we have not changed!

The reasons for this are not difficult to understand. *Metanoia* is *self*-denial. The forfeiture of that human quest for control and independence is precisely the dynamic of all secular attempts at community. *Authentic community comes, like life itself, as a gift.*[9] From the human side, its possibility can only be stated in a paradox—the death of self (ego) in order to live in the wholeness of personhood, or the loss of independent individual life (psyche) in order to find it in the interdependence of community. *Metanoia* means *submission* to God as "the Lord." It cannot be understood as a causative factor in the creation of community but only as a receptive one. Thus it affronts the aggressive instincts of secular man who has not experienced the reality of creative receptivity.

In summary, *metanoia* is response to the work of God in the human personality and society. Secular humanity considers such a possibility, quite literally, nonsense and therefore outside the realm of human operation. *Metanoia* is the recognition that authentic community is not the creation of human knowledge and power, any more than health is created by antisepsis or surgery. In the words of the prophet Zechariah, "Not by might, nor by power, but by my Spirit, says the Lord of Hosts" (4:6). Community is created by God's Spirit and received in repentance.

The psychological and social implications of this are significant. The recognition of community as gift informs the experience with grace. It transforms the posture of individual response from constraint to privilege, and from acquisitiveness to sharing. Community is a gift to be appreciated through participation, not a right to be demanded from others.

Koinonia—the New Pattern

When we speak of authentic community we are not referring to one social or political system over against another. Our concern is not as such with socialism versus capitalism, democracy in contrast to monarchy, or a parliamentary versus a presidential system. These systems are of the world, all built on the fundamental presupposition that self-interest is the commanding principle. Neither is it our primary intent to define the precise social structure for a given Christian community. Authentic community can take different social and economic forms.[10] What concerns us is the inner form, that is, the quality and dynamic of relationship which must animate and shape any human social system in order to be humane, reflecting the "image of God."

In the New Testament the inner forms of the two alternative human communities—the "old" and the "new"—are contrasted with a variety of descriptive analogies. The one is the *old creation,* where "death reigns" (Rom. 5:14). The other is the *new creation,* where the power of life creates "righteousness and true holiness" (Eph. 4:22–24). In the old creation, the "principalities and powers" rule by the threat of death. In the new, the Spirit of Christ governs by breaking the old vicious cycle of sin and death.[11]

The contrast between the "old," which is the product of human ingenuity and force, and the "new," or the original community as renewed in Christ, can be seen at a glance in the following chart.

THE COMMUNITIES CHARACTERIZED

Old ("Law")	New ("Spirit")

Presupposition:
1) "In *Adam*" — self-interest or *ego* centrism
2) *Idios* — private property

1) "In Christ" — bear each other's burdens."
2) *Koinos* — openness, sharing, "unity of heart and soul."

Dynamic:
1) *Eros* — desire for that which appeals to and enhances the self
2) Competition — struggle for independence and self-aggrandizement

1) *Agape* — response to the other as intrinsically worthy whether desirable or not.
2) *Koinonia* — interdependence and equitable distribution according to need.

Control:
1) "Legal statute" — prohibits destructive, selfish action

2) "Balance of power" — power of self-defense, "eye for eye and tooth for tooth"
3) "Enlightenment" — to know what is in one's best self-interest; thus enlightened self-restraint

1) "Spirit of Christ" ("fruit of Spirit" — against such there is no law).
2) "Law of love" — overcome evil with good; never avenge yourselves.
3) "Response to grace" — We love because God first loved us. "Love is the fulfilling of the law." Gratitude.

Character of goodness:
1) "Works" — disciplined self-effort to achieve merit
2) "Altruism" or "Benevolence" —I share what is *mine.*

1) *Metanoia* and "faith" — free response to gift
2) *Shalom* — We share God's gifts — *agapeic justice.*

The old community is "in *Adam*"; the new is "in Christ." *Adam* represents the egocentric principle of "old nature" which grasps for knowledge and power in order to achieve the image of God through human exertion (Col. 3:5–9). *Christ* represents the "new nature." He is the "second *Adam*," the "man from heaven," who received the authentic image through submission to God's covenant. He is the "man from heaven" who is both "life-giving spirit" and the pattern or image for the human family ("those who are of the dust").[13]

To be "in Christ," therefore, means to reject egocentrism as the original fact of one's being, and to live in the new reality of God-centeredness (Gal. 2:20). This is neither the metaphor of Christ mysticism nor the human psychology of altruism. What Paul describes in Galatians 2:20 and 3:27–28, for example, is a new psychological and social principle which informs authentic community.[14] This is the new orientation which radically alters one's perspective on life and its values (2 Cor. 5:16–17), and changes the pattern of relations to one's fellows.

In the old order, goodness has the character of "works," that is, achievement through disciplined self-effort according to a rule. Virtue is a habit acquired through practice, according to Aristotle. "Practice makes perfect" is an adage from the Greeks. And righteousness is a precise regimen following legal precepts, according to the Jewish Pharisees. In the new order, by contrast, goodness is the spontaneous expression of the reorientation (*metanoia*) and the new Spirit/spirit which has been received. The New Testament word for this kind of goodness is *"faith."* This goodness comes by participating in the "faithfulness of Christ" (Gal. 2:16–17).[15] Paul also uses the metaphor of slave and child in the home to accentuate this difference of perspective for acceptable behavior. The slave behaves under compulsion; the child responds in "freedom," which does not mean perfectly, because it belongs to the family.[16]

Perhaps the most decisive psychological distinction made by New Testament writers is that between the principle of *idios* and *koinos* (Acts 2:44; 4:32–33). *Idios* is the principle of atomistic individualism and self-centeredness. In the order of *idios*, the ego defines its domain of rights and possessions in terms of self-interest and private control. One individual relates to another competitively and with an eye to self-aggrandizement. In its extremity, it leads to narcissism and the attitude of Cain (1 John 3:12), who rejected responsibility for his brother.

Koinos is the principle of commonality and interdependence. What we share in common, for example light, air, and language, is *koinos*. In the order of *koinos* there is an interrelatedness of give and take in the knowledge of our common dependence.

Koinos includes but goes beyond altruism, that is, unselfish concern for others. Altruism points to sharing as *giving*, as an outer or other-directedness which assumes the sufficiency and independence of the altruistic individual. Indeed, Aristotle pointed out that one cannot be generous, or altruistic, unless one has plentitude of wealth! *Koinos* points to sharing as *participation*—both giving and receiving in mutual interdependence. "Bear each other's burdens and so fulfill the law of Christ," wrote St. Paul (Gal. 6:2). The movement of serving and being served, of giving and receiving, is a constant alternation between the self and the other, the I and Thou. The order of Christian *koinonia* is based upon the recognition of the commonality of our life in Jesus Christ and our mutual need of each other.

Christian Agape

The New Testament concept of love *(agape)*, which is the dynamic of the new community, is uniquely portrayed in Christ. *Agape* is first of all God's love, and as a gift of the Creator it is the "image of God" in the creature. It is, thus, the *original* spiritual form ("the Word") guiding human community in the creation—the divine possibility of love creating authentic human relationship. Indeed, from the biblical perspective the creation can only be understood as a labor of love. *Agape* is the very dynamic of life and goodness, the creative urge for participation and personal relationship in authentic community.

But in sinful human experience, *agape* is first known as *forgiving love*, or *grace*, which is received and shared in the posture of *metanoia*. Mankind's "original" sin was and is the rejection of *agape* as the way of life. We have substituted self-centered desire as the dynamic center for community. For that reason *agape* has to be reintroduced as a human possibility through the redeeming love manifested in the life and death of Jesus, the Christ. The words of John, "We love because he first loved us," apply with equal validity to God's acts both in creation and redemption.

The word *eros* has been used by some theologians and ethical philosophers to denote the self-centered human impulse, and they set it in the sharpest contrast to *agape*.[18] The contrast is apparent, but should not be pressed to the point of sheer contradiction and mutual exclusion. *Eros* is not the devil, although it may become demonic when its claims are given unqualified recognition.[19]

But before we can discuss the nature of *eros* further, we must correct two prevalent misconceptions. *Eros* is not equated with sex. The contrast between *eros* and *agape* is not between physical or sensual love and spiritual longing. In the Greek Bible (both the Septuagint and New Testament), *agape* is used to cover the whole spectrum of human relationships.[20] Second, the contrast is not between self-negation or repression and self-affirmation and acceptance. *Agape* affirms the worth of the self as God's good creature and seeks fellowship in authentic community.

Eros is desire for possession and enjoyment of the beloved object.[21] It directs the self toward possession of the desirable object, whether that object be person or thing, physical or spiritual, as the way to self-fulfillment. And in this is its fatal flaw: it is essentially a self-centered impulse. Such attraction or desire for self-fulfillment through possessive union—possessing and being possessed—is precisely the door through which the first temptation entered.

While not in itself evil, *eros* is inadequate as the comprehensive principle for organizing community. The desire for self-enhancement and fulfillment is not in itself evil, but when the self and its desires become the primary psychological and ethical center of reference, life goes askew. A demonic *eros* corrupts the use of power. It turns creative work into competitive labor, and diverts the production of life's necessities into the exploitation of the earth's resources for private profit and wasteful self-defense. It prostitutes the sexual experience, changing it from a relationship to an act of self-gratification.[22] Even the quest for spirituality, the "heavenly *eros*," may become self-centered and callous to the needs of others!

Such a circumstance provides no alternative to regulating the individual by legal prohibitions enforced with physical coercion. The freedom of *agape* is given up for the bondage of law. The image of a son is transmuted into the image of a slave.

Agape, which was rejected in the first instance, again becomes a possibility through its embodiment in Jesus Christ. It is not an abstract spiritual ideal, an "impossible possibility," as Reinhold Niebuhr put it.[23] Neither is it a "counsel of perfection," which a few saints might attain by strenuous discipline. It again enters our human experience of community as a gift of God which offers the divine possibility of freedom through love. A "new creation," it transforms the selfish center of desire—the demonic *eros*—and creates anew the real possibility for authentic relationships.

Agape enriches and extends human love. It does not reject or deny the sensual and emotional, but rather ennobles and gives the quality of genuine *koinonia* to such relationships. It extends the natural affections of friendship beyond the immediate boundaries of family, tribe, or national group. It does not cancel out mutuality *(philia)*, but extends it to include the enemy within the bonds of mutuality. "Enemy" can no longer be defined as one for whom I have no responsibility. *Agape* requires identical good will toward all persons.

Loving "in Christ"

As a Christian concept, *agape* has a distinct character which is expressed by the phrase "in Christ." For example, Christians speak of loving each other and all mankind "in Christ." Or they sometimes claim that *agape* is only possible "in Christ." What do these kinds of statements mean? Is *agape* possible only for Christians?

First a caution is necessary. This phrase, strictly speaking, is jargon or inside language of Christians, and we need both to understand what it means and be careful in our use of it. It does not mean that those "outside of Christ" are not loved, or that they are loved only because Jesus asks us to ("for Jesus' sake"). That would imply that they are not loved in and for themselves, and may leave the impression that we do not consider them worth loving. But by its very nature, *agape* is a response to each person for his or her own sake. Those who are loved "in Christ" are regarded for their own sake. What, then, does this expression mean? What is the relation of Christ to *agape* as the inner form of authentic community?

The phrase "in Christ" qualifies the concept of love in the same way that the meaning of comrade is modified in the phrase "comrade in arms." The phrase "in arms" suggests that the camaraderie has a penultimate character, that is, the comradeship is not in and for itself, but in and for a cause. But if we make *agape* less than an end in itself, does this not inevitably debase its genuine character? When someone is loved in Christ, does it mean that he is loved for some extraneous reason? How shall we explain this penultimate character of *agape* for others?

The first part of the answer to this question is that the ultimate reality "in Christ" is not extraneous to *agape*. To follow our analogy used above, the cause in which comrades are joined materially affects the quality of their relationship. For example, to be partners in crime suggests a qualitatively different relationship than to be partners in sports or business. If *agape* is penultimate to an end which contradicts its nature or negates its possibilities, then, of course, it is debased. However, if the end is intrinsic to and complements the relation, then it will enhance the individual who loves and heighten the quality of the relationship.

But further, *agape* in the biblical sense is a relationship "under God," that is, under covenant, and is qualified by the recognition that the *self*—myself and yourself—is not the ultimate end. *Agape* is not a purely humanistic concept. It does not divinize the self. Self is always penultimate to God who has been revealed "in Christ." Thus the one loved is never idolized.

This must be considered in the formation of human

community. To what or whom are individual persons ultimately subject? Only to their own inner selves as individualism holds? In that case the ego is given that status of the divine. Or is the self subject to collective humanity, or some reprensentative part of it such as family or nation? In that case the ego is subjected to its own inflated image, and the national ego, the family as divine ancestors, or "Humanity" is given divine status.

The Christian answer is that the human ego and relationships are penultimate to God as he was disclosed in Christ. God is love. That means that he is the Ultimate Reality and Cause which gives authenticity to human relationships. Therefore he has the intrinsic right or authority to define the terms of the covenant under which mankind lives. Christians believe that he has done this "in Christ."

In summary, then, the qualification "in Christ" means that the source of *agape* is the God whom Christ revealed. He disclosed to us *God's* love (John 3:16) as the creative, redeeming source of all life and love. Further, *agape* is that kind of love which is seen most clearly in Jesus himself. Having an historical point of reference, it is not a mythical or ethical ideal beyond human possibility, but has already become historical reality in Jesus Christ.

This *agape* is realized in our lives through sharing in the love of Christ. It comes to us not only as an historical revelation through him but as a continuing possibility in his fellowship. "We [can] love because he first loved us."[24] This is a demonstrated psychological principle in all human relationships, which the Christian recognizes must apply in the first instance to the Christ because he is the revelation of *agape*. This is the psychological meaning of the theological statement that love is God's gift to us in Christ.

This clearly implies that one gets no brownie points for *agape*. Self-congratulation is inconsistent with love. The beloved person has worth "in Christ," that is, not as one who is desirable to me, *but as having worth* independently of any immediate advantage to me. Because the beloved is worthy of love, there is no self-congratulation in loving.

Lastly, to be "in Christ" means in the New Testament to

be "in the body" or community of Christ. Thus, to love in Christ means to regard the other person as a fellow member or potentially a fellow member of the authentic community (Eph. 2:13–22). Here we must specifically note that the "in Christ" relationship is not a matter of religious camaraderie or bias in favor of co-religionists. *Agape* is the love of God *for the world* which was demonstrated in Christ. In him it has become available for authentic *human* community, not just "Christian" religious community. The single universal condition is *metanoia*.

Thus to love "in Christ" is the mission and witness of the church (2 Cor. 5:14–15). Christ sent his disciples into the world as the Father had sent him. To be in his body, that is, "in him," is to be joined in his mission of the reconciliation of all mankind to God.

Notes to Chapter V

1. Early Christians were referred to as a "third race." Note "Jews, Greeks, and Church of God" (1 Cor. 10:32), and "one new humanity" (Eph. 2:15).

2. Dietrich Bonhoeffer, *The Way to Freedom*, Harper & Row, 1966, p. 46.

3. Martin Buber, *I and Thou*, Scribners, 1958.

4. In this and the following analysis of community I am indebted to Bonhoeffer's insights in *The Communion of Saints*, Harper & Row, 1963, pp. 53ff.

5. See for example Alan Richardson, *An Introduction to the Theology of the New Testament*, Harper & Row, 1958, pp. 31–34. Bonhoeffer is quite correct to link this act of repentance to being caught up in the messianic event. The mission of the community is already implied in its "repentance." See *Letters and Papers from Prison*, Macmillan, 1967, pp. 190–91.

6. See Floyd Filson, *A Commentary on the Gospel According to St. Matthew*, Harper & Row, 1960, pp. 68ff.

7. Psalm 37, to which the third beatitude (Matt. 5:5) alludes, describes the "wicked" as striving, angry, aggressive, and impatient. They do not have the grace of acceptance.

8. Is China's revolution, with its built-in process of self-criticism and continuing revolution, a secular version of repentance?

9. Eberhard Arnold, founder of the Society of Brothers, constantly stressed this in his writings.

10. In the Reformation era, the Hutterites argued that a communal style was the only pattern that fully qualified as Christian community. They defined true Christian love and yieldedness to God as renouncing private property. But other Anabaptist groups defined commonality as willingness to put one's goods at the brotherhood's disposal when needed, and they left room for individual ownership and management of property. See the "Congregational Order" in *The Legacy of Michael Sattler,* Herald Press, 1976, p. 45.

11. See Phillips' translation of Romans 8:2–4.

12. Paul Minear has developed a similar contrast of the old and new age in his article, "The Vocation of the Church: Some Exegetical Clues," *Missiology* (Jan., 1977), p. 25. This article came to my attention after my own analysis was already completed.

13. See 1 Cor. 15:45–49; Phil. 2:5–11; Col. 1:15; 3:9–11.

14. The "in Christ" category has long been debated. On the one hand, see James Stewart, *A Man in Christ,* Harper (n.d.), who tends to underscore Deissmann's "Christ mysticism"; and on the other, Eric Wahlstrom, *The New Life in Christ,* Muhlenberg, 1950, who stresses its moral dimensions.

15. The literal phrase here is not "faith in Christ," but "the faithfulness of Christ." Paul says that we are not justified by our works but by his faithfulness.

16. See the tract, "On Two Kinds of Obedience," attributed to Michael Sattler, a sixteenth-century Anabaptist martyr. Sattler contrasts "servile and filial" obedience (*Legacy of Michael Sattler, op. cit.,* pp. 121ff.). This tract makes an interesting comparison to Luther's "two kinds of righteousness."

17. For a comparative study of the meaning of *eros, philia,* and *agape,* see my *The Community of the Spirit,* Eerdmans, 1974, chapter 5, "The Spirit of Love."

18. Anders Nygren, *Eros and Agape,* Westminster, 1953; and Karl Barth, *Church Dogmatics,* T. & T. Clark, 1956, especially IV/2, p. 740. Both of these theologians tend to make the distinction an absolute contradiction.

19. "But Eros, honoured without reservation and obeyed unconditionally, becomes a demon. And this is just how he claims to be honoured and obeyed. Divinely indifferent to our selfishness, he is also demoniacally rebellious to every claim of God or Man

that would oppose him." C. S. Lewis, *The Four Loves*, Harcourt Brace, 1960, p. 154.

20. See William E. Phipps, "The Sensuousness of Agape," *Theology Today* (Jan., 1973), pp. 370–79; see also William Lillie, "The Christian Conception of Love," *Studies in New Testament Ethics*, Oliver and Boyd, 1961, pp. 163–81.

21. Rollo May has an insightful analysis of *eros* as human dynamic in his *Love and Will*, Delta, 1969. See especially pp. 72–98. Also, Gordon Allport deals helpfully with the concepts of self-extension and self-enhancement in his chapter "The Proprium," in *Becoming*, Yale, 1955, pp. 41–56.

22. Making the distinction between sex and *eros*, C. S. Lewis wrote, "Sexual desire, without Eros, wants *it*, the *thing in itself*; Eros wants the Beloved. The *thing* is a sensory pleasure; that is, an event occurring within one's own body." *Op. cit.*, p. 134.

23. Reinhold Niebuhr, *The Interpretation of Christian Ethics*, Harper, 1935.

24. This is certainly the gist of the passage in 1 John 4:7–21.

VI

THE CHURCH AS A SIGN IN PROTESTANT THEOLOGY

Hᴏᴡ ɪꜱ ᴛʜᴇ ᴄʜᴜʀᴄʜ ᴛᴏ ʙᴇ "ɪɴ ᴛʜᴇ ᴡᴏʀʟᴅ"? ᴛʜᴀᴛ is the question! In his extended prayer on the eve of his crucifixion, Jesus spoke of his disciples as those whom the Father had given him "out of the world." They were to be a community of witness whose earthly origin ("out of the world") was no longer their authenticating origin. The Father had *given them* to him to continue his mission, and they were, like himself, no longer "of the world." They were being consecrated with his own authenticating hallmark ("glory") and sent "into the world" even as he himself had been sent into the world to continue his presence and witness (John 17:6–19).

This is John's way of describing the position of the church in the world. But what does it mean for life-style and strategy? Why did he not spell it out in more programmatic language? Did it all seem so obvious in his situation that further description seemed unnecessary? Perhaps he left such questions unanswered because they can only be answered by each continuing generation in its own time and place under the guidance of the Spirit.

For a thousand years after the church had become "established" under the mandates of the Roman emperors, the answer to our question seemed clear. The church should exist in the world as the spiritual counterpart of the political organization of the empire. It was organized accordingly as a universal religious institution with lines of authority legally legitimized to exercise power over the spiritual and moral aspects of life in the world. While the Reformation challenged the limits and grounds of the church's authority, it did not directly challenge the fundamental idea of the church as the institutional counterpart to the political government. Not until the modern period, when the implications of the Reformation and the Renaissance had worked themselves out in the formation of "free churches," secular states, and pluralistic societies, did the question of the church's life and relevance in the world emerge as an urgent, self-conscious inquiry for Protestants.

The Church Invisible

American evangelicalism, the heir of orthodoxy, has given very little theological attention to the question of the nature of the visible church in the world. Beyond the assertion that the church is made up of believers and should be free from political controls, it has simply drawn upon the classical concepts of a "professing" (visible) church, and the confessing or true church which is invisible.[1] The shape of the contemporary Protestant discussion about the church as a sign in and to the world stems mainly from the more recent influence of Karl Barth and neo-biblical studies.

Although legal establishment was abolished by the federal Constitution, evangelical Protestantism in America has assumed a place in society that has been dubbed "social establishment." Further, it has assumed that the nation, rather than the church itself, was the carrier of God's purposes in history. The church was viewed as a supporting institution upholding the morals and religious convictions of the nation, through organized revivals and evangelistic campaigns, Sunday Schools, the forming of denominational colleges, and voluntary societies such as temperance unions, to influence public life and morals. The revivals, along with regular Sunday worship, aimed to maintain the individuals in their Christian commitment. Other religious and quasi-religious organizations aimed at political influence and indirect control.

The church's self-image as a "true church" was spiritualized, individualized, and interiorized. Elect individuals who gained salvation by acceptance of orthodox doctrines of sin, and salvation through faith, might have inner assurance of God's grace, but they did not view themselves as a corporate, visible true church. And since individual salvation was directly related to correct theological belief, evangelicalism's major concern was to protect the message of the church from error and to preach an evangelistic message to the world.

This lack of emphasis on the identity and role of the church as a corporate witness in the world is quite understandable in light of the history of Protestant theology. Reformed orthodoxy spoke of the true church as invisible—a dubious quality for a good sign.[2] Speaking for Lutheranism, Melanchthon avoided the term "invisible" because it seemed to justify the taunts of their critics that Lutherans had a "Platonic church." His substitute phrasing, however, did not change the concept implied in an invisible true church. His visible professing church was one in which "the true saints and heirs of eternal life" are not readily visible among the many "hypocrites and ungodly people" who are making confession in this visible company.[3]

The word and sacraments were the "external signs" of the invisible spiritual reality in which the visible church participated and by virtue of which it also could be called "true." The visible life of the church as an authentic community of disciples was not the significant reality.

Nor was the orthodoxy of an earlier age likely to consider the church as a sign of the *kingdom* since it was, on the whole, not millennialist. Melanchthon clearly rejected a millennial kingdom as a Judaistic and Anabaptist heresy. William Ames, the great Puritan divine, identified the true church, that is, in its invisible modality, with the kingdom of God or the kingdom of Christ indifferently. In both cases the kingdom was conceived as spiritual and eternal. The true church was this reality in "mystical" form, and not a sign of an historical reality which was yet future. The true church was a spiritual end in itself which would be perfected and manifested at the second advent of Christ.[4]

The question of the church's witness in the world was treated as the individual Christian's role in society. The church was conceptualized as a religious society over against the civil and political community, whose role it was to maintain true doctrine and right administration of the sacraments. It had a specialized religious role. The lay Christian's spiritual life was nourished in the church, but he lived and witnessed in the civil community, fulfilling his Christian vocation there. Thus, again, the church itself was not understood as authentic community witnessing to the covenant intention of God for the whole of human community.

Dispensationalism, which played a formative part in the theology of American fundamentalism and thus influenced evangelicalism, exaggerated the invisibility and irrelevancy of the church as a sign of God's covenant purpose. It put the kingdom back into an historical setting as the future and final stage of God's saving work in history, but it interpreted it as a Jewish reality fulfilling the promise made to Israel. The church, a Gentile phenomenon, is a "parenthesis" in kingdom strategy. Thus the church has little or nothing to do with the kingdom either as agent or sign.

The kingdom of God is a future social reality in dispensationalist theology, but the church is purely spiritual. Its visible role (not only its inner form) is spiritualized. It is to be concerned only with the inward spiritual condition and standing of individuals, and so has no inherent social role or value as a sign of the kingdom.

During the decade of the 1970s, a significant challenge to this individualistic and spiritualistic view of salvation and the church has appeared with the emergence of the Church Growth movement within evangelicalism. Advocates of church growth have insisted that the goal of evangelism and missions is "multiplication of *cells* of reborn Christians," that is, churches, and not simply saved individuals.[5] Theologians of this movement have also begun to reassociate the church with the future triumphant reign of Christ. The church is not in any sense a direct cause or agent of the kingdom, but as a part of God's redemptive mission in the world, which will eventuate in Christ's return, it has relevance as witness to it. The church is reinstated to the center of God's redemptive purpose in this age, but its exact relation to the kingdom, which will be directly ushered in by Christ's return, is not entirely clear in Church Growth theology.

Howard Snyder, who by and large espouses the Church Growth position, gives us perhaps the clearest statement of the significance of the church for the kingdom. In his most recent book, *The Community of the King* (1977), he defines the kingdom as "the progressive extension of God's reign over all creation,"[6] and he maintains that the kingdom as well as the church is to grow. The kingdom which has appeared in Jesus Christ "is now present implicitly in the Church, is at work secretly in the world and will come in true, creative, restoring and judging power when Jesus Christ returns to earth." Thus he concludes, "When the Church is truly prophetic, it advances the cause of the Kingdom. And when it is both prophetic and evangelistic, it is true to the Kingdom. Then church growth means kingdom growth."

Snyder's work clearly reflects the influence of South American theologians like Orlando Costas[7] and other so-called liberation theologies. His forthright rejection of older dispensationalist categories and implications will undoubtedly stir up new discussion and debate in evangelical circles.

Karl Barth's Concept

As we noted, Karl Barth's concept of the church as a sign of God's purpose in and for the world generated new themes in the discussion of ecclesiology. In many respects the description of his theology as a *new (neo-)*orthodoxy is particularly appropriate to his doctrine of the church. While he returns to Luther and Calvin for his dominant emphasis, he is also generally faithful to the basic themes of Post-Reformation orthodoxy. He has dealt with the doctrine of the church at various points in his theology, but is always quite self-consciously countering the moralistic, activistic, social, and political concepts of liberal theology.

While Barth in every context spoke of the church as a visible historical reality, his dominant concern was to reassert its spiritual or theocentric dimension (its "third dimension"), in which the "invisible Lord and His invisible Spirit" are acknowledged to be the creative source and authority for its life.[8] Perhaps his characteristic word "event," which he also used to describe the church, best captures the multidimensional quality of his concept.[9] First, to say that the church is an event denies that it is a religious society constituted by human piety and organization. It happens *in response* to what the living Christ is doing. Jesus Christ through his Holy Spirit initiates the action that creates the church as an event. Second, the word "event" underscores the visible, historical reality of the church. "The church," he wrote, "*is* when it takes place."[10] The church as "the living community of the living Lord Jesus Christ" is a visible reality.

The external form of this event is the gathering (*ekklēsia*). The church exists primarily as a *congregation* gathered in worship and proclamation of Jesus Christ as Lord and Savior of the world. In his contribution to the World Council of Churches' symposium, *Man's Disorder and God's Design*, he wrote:

> The primary, normal, and visible form of this event is the *local congregation* meeting in a 'parish' or 'district' with clearly defined boundaries. . . . The Church lives (she *is*) in this visible, concrete, transaction (prayer, confession of faith, Baptism, Lord's Supper, the proclamation and reception of the Gospel), and in its presuppositions (theology, training of the young), and its consequences (brotherly discipline, pastoral care and other oversight).[11]

Barth also constantly called this congregation a community (*Gemeinde*), and he acknowledged that it has the usual characteristics of human communities—human fellowship, organized authority, "patterns of community life and divisions of labor."[12] But he insisted that while the church *exists* in the form of human community, it *consists* alone by the creative action of the Holy Spirit. The "living community" can never be unequivocally identified with its human manifestations. Only by faith does the church perceive itself to be the work of God through the Holy Spirit. On its human side as visible community, it is only an "analogy" and an imperfect "manifestation" of the true spiritual reality. In its temporal existence the true *"being of the community"* is hidden under considerable and very powerful appearances to the contrary.[13]

For these reasons Barth did not speak of the church as God's agent. He preferred words like sign, representative, and witness. In fact, when he wrote of the church as sign in the first volume of the *Church Dogmatics,* he wrote with guarded precision. The church as such is not the sign, but rather the church *in the event of preaching and hearing the Word.* He wrote, "Therefore the sign, too, set up in the Church, *of the Bible somehow speaking and being heard,* is a genuine sign, but nonetheless, also, no more than that."[14] Note the careful qualifications: a "genuine" *sign,* but *only* a sign. Further, the sign is not something that the congregation does or is, even in response to the preaching. The proclamation and invitation to faith is in no sense a "fulfilment that has already happened." Very precisely, then, the sign is the event of the Bible being heard as the Word of God in the midst of the congregation, and not some continuing effect of that experience in the life of the community.

Does the life of the community in its structure and daily relationships have no value as a sign? From the above, one might well conclude that it is minimal! But in his discussion of the work of the Holy Spirit as sanctifier, Barth suggests that the community exists as a *"provisional representation"* of the sanctification of all humanity and human life which God intends in the kingdom.[15] What does this *"provisional representation"* imply? We need not guess because he spells it out at some length.

In the first place, to say "representation" means that the community knows and shares *"de facto,"* not only in Christ's work of justification (forgiveness and cancellation of guilt), but also in the sanctification ("the elevation and establish-ment") of all humanity which God accomplished *"de jure"* in the resurrection and exaltation of Christ. The Christian community is the "holy community of the intervening period" between the first and second advents.[16] As holy community, it bears witness to the work of God which is proceeding toward its final manifestation in Jesus Christ.

In the second place, it means that the Christian commu-nity is not an end in itself. As a *provisional* representation, it is both an indication of the end or goal toward which God is moving history and a movement in the direction of that end. The goal of the community, then, is not to be the true church, that is, a perfect or unequivocal representation. This is Barth's word against perfectionism. He makes this specific. The community is provisional because it has not achieved and will not achieve sanctification. "It can only attest it in the puzzling form of a reflection (1 Cor. 13:12)."[17] As a sign it is "fragmentary and incomplete and insecure and questionable."

Barth is very cautious lest the church make "pretentious claims" and in the end express and reveal only the "semblance of a church." "This," he wrote, "is the particular sin which to some extent is always committed where the community arises and continues here and now."[18] The warn-ing is well taken, but when fear of the sin of commission leads to a sin of omission, shall we not be judged by the words of Jesus against the fearful servant who hid his talents in the ground until his master returned? The sign may func-tion as a sign if it is "fragmentary and incomplete." But when it is "insecure and questionable," then its credibility as a sign is called into question!

Last, the term indicates that the church is not a causal factor in the arrival of the kingdom. The end *(eschaton)*, of which it is a provisional sign, is "not the result of its own existence," but something completely new which is given to it, something which comes to it from God. The church in building up itself does not thereby build up the kingdom of God.[19] The consummation of God's purposes for history, like the individual's justification and sanctification, comes as a gift of grace. Surely every authentic community of witness must take seriously this warning against triumphalism and over-confidence.

Barth's final word to us, then, is that the sign is the church gathered to hear the Word. If we ask what authenticates or gives credibility to the sign, we are told that it is self-authenticating. Here Barth restates the Reformers' doctrine of the inward witness of the Holy Spirit, but denies the later orthodox theory of verbal inspiration as an authenticating mark. By the same token there are no direct authenticating marks in the life of the congregation.[20] The only truly *visible* sign is the act of preaching itself, which seems to practically reduce the concept of sign to arbitrary symbol. Thus the significance of the community's life in the Spirit as an authenticating witness is greatly minimized.

Ecumenical Directions

Bonhoeffer's influence is also reflected in ecumenical Protestantism's discussion of the church's identity and role in the world. We shall speak of this at more length in the last chapter, but his concepts had an important effect on the nuance of meaning implied in the word "sign."

Bonhoeffer's early theological orientation was very similar to Barth's; indeed, it owed much to him. However, in his earlier books such as *Communion of Saints, The Cost of Discipleship,* and *Life Together,* he gave much more attention to the shape and nature of community. He insisted that community is the "new creation"—that part of the world which has been made new—and he emphasized the obedience which the church owes to her Lord. This latter point was especially etched in his mind by the necessity of the break with the German Christians, who accepted Hitler as a legitimate leader, and the formation of the Confessing Church. Obedience for him finally meant martyrdom ("costly grace").

Bonhoeffer's distinctive contribution to the concept of the church as a sign in the world was his accent on the church "for the world." His theology focused on God's activity in Christ for the world. Jesus was "the Man for others," and the risen Christ is lord over the whole world of men and things. The world is the sphere of God's saving activity, and the church is a part of that world—a significant part. His theology was self-consciously Christocentric and "secular," in contrast to "church-centric" and religious.

When the ecumenical conversation appropriated these themes from Bonhoeffer, its discussion gradually shifted from the nature of the church in the world to the nature of God's work in the world. The older slogan, "Let the Church be the Church!" was in effect displaced by a new one, "Let the Church be for the world." During this phase of the discussion the word "secular" became a slogan for ecumenical theology, and the role of the church as a religious institution was by implication, if not intent, downgraded. True, there was some talk about *The Secular Congregation* (Robert Raines, 1967), and the "Church scattered" as well as gathered (Hans-Ruedi Weber, *Salty Christians*, 1963), but earlier voices speaking about *God's Colony in Man's World* (George Webber, 1960) and the essentially secular significance of the liturgy (John A. T. Robinson, *Liturgy Coming to Life*, 1960) were muted. The urgent questions became, "What is God doing *in the world?*" and "What role, if any, does the church play in this?"[21]

The answer to these questions reverted by and large to the traditional Protestant distinction between the lay and clerical functions in the church.[22] The real burden of God's mission in the world falls on the shoulders of the layman whose life is *in the world*. Indeed, greatly increased importance was given to the vocation of lay witness in the "real world"; and the result was that the organized Christian community took on the traditional character of a *religious* sign.

The sign was interpreted as the congregation gathered in worship, and more particularly gathered around the Lord's table. According to this theology, when the congregation is gathered in confession to receive grace through the sacraments, it bears witness to the true source of mankind's life in the grace of God. Thus gathered around *one* table of the

Lord, the church becomes a sign of that coming unity of mankind which is God's goal for history in Jesus Christ. This gathering is a clue to the hidden meaning of God's activity in and for the world.

In this sense the church is "sacramental," but by defining its sacramental life in essentially liturgical terms the sign becomes strictly a religious one. The exciting possible implications of Barth's concept of the church as the "inner circle" who recognize and obey Christ as Lord of the whole world, and of Bonhoeffer's community as that part of the world made new in Christ, were not followed through. The church was not recognized as authentic community—an actual new "secular" beginning and sign in the midst of the old—which can be a continuing demonstration of the power of God in its life together.

One is repeatedly disappointed by the way in which the grand statements about the church as the new reality seem to evaporate into religious symbolism when they are given an operational interpretation! Take for example the following statement from the Fourth World Conference on Faith and Order (1963): "The Church is the 'new creation' precisely as the body of the crucified-risen Lord. Even as Christ's glory is revealed in his self-humiliation, so in Christ the Church is called and enabled to manifest the 'new creation' in obedient discipleship and faithful servanthood in the world." When interpreted, however, this means that Christians should take their secular vocations seriously as obedience to Christ and that the church should "make Christ present again and again through proclamation of the word and administration of the sacraments."[23]

The Church as Sacrament of the Kingdom

There is a sense in which we need to speak of the authentic community itself as a sacrament. Sacrament means the visible sign of the reality of Christ's presence by grace. To be a sacrament the sign must be authentic. It must have the intrinsic quality of the original—the *authentēs*. There must be a recognizable reality which marks it as genuine or it loses its credibility as sign, becoming an arbitrary symbol, not a sacrament.

The presence of Jesus Christ becomes a sacramental reality to the world in and through the new creation of authentic community (Acts 2:44–45; 4:32f.). It is recognized in the attitude of the community *(metanoia)* and in the spirit and order of the life together *(agape* and *koinonia).* The *life of the community* is sacramental. What are usually called "the sacraments" are the ceremonial celebrations of that sacramental life. Baptism is the ceremony of initiation. The eucharist, which means thanksgiving, is the celebration of the communion *(koinonia)* experienced in the life of brotherhood. If the reality is not present, the ceremony is empty and becomes not a blessing but a judgment (1 Cor. 11:29). Where the new life of *koinonia* is reality, the ceremony becomes a visible manifestation *to the community itself* of Christ's presence. The ceremony alone cannot function as an effective sign *to the world.*[24]

This demand for a new social reality as sacramental sign dare not be compromised in the name of preserving a high doctrine of grace. The church is more than a "voice in the wilderness" proclaiming justification by faith. Like its master, it is a demonstration of the new faith-righteousness. The church is more than the keeper of the sacraments by which grace may be administered to sinners. The new community is not merely a group of penitents constantly making confession and receiving forgiveness, but a fellowship of the reconciled. It is the firstfruits of the new creation, the "body of Christ."

The use of the analogy of "body" for both the church and the bread of the Lord's Supper is hardly casual coincidence. The apostle's solemn warning to the Corinthian Christians (1 Cor. 11:20–32), that the "unworthy manner" of their communion is a profaning of the body and blood of the Lord, ties the actual life of the community and the celebration of the Lord's Supper together in the closest sacramental unity. The "unworthy manner" referred to was the rude, unbrotherly manner of their celebration in which they "despised the church of God" and humiliated the poor. This self-contradicting inconsistency was what led Paul to say that they were eating their own supper and not the Lord's.

Authentic witness requires us to move beyond the realm of the rational idea which can be preserved in orthodox confessions, and verbally proclaimed by evangelistic preaching. It demands that we move beyond the expression of personal piety and reverence for the ceremonial symbolism of the great ecumenical tradition. We must move beyond the language of interior, individual experience to the social dimension of the new reality "in Christ." It is not fundamentally a question of religious observance ("circumcision") or the lack of it ("uncircumcision"), but the reality of "faith working through love" (Gal. 5:6).

Therefore we must move beyond the programmatic language of evangelism *and* service, worship *and* secular vocation, faith *and* works. Theologically and experientially in the life of the community, discipleship must be understood as the gift of grace along with faith-belief. The disciple-in-community is God's creative sign—his "poem" (Eph. 2:10). Authentic discipleship *is* sacramental. Faith *is* active in love. Love, insofar as it participates in the love of Christ, is a gift, and as such becomes the sacramental sign.

Notes to Chapter VI

1. The chapter "Christ and His Church," in *Fundamentals of the Faith* (ed. by C. F. H. Henry, Zondervan, 1969), which was to be a contemporary statement of evangelical faith by leading scholars, is simply a restatement of classical Protestant theology both in its language and the issues considered.

2. William Ames, a seventeenth-century Puritan theologian, is typical in his usage: "Invisibility is a condition or mode of the church having to do with its essential and internal form; visibility is a condition or mode of the church having to do with its accidental or outward form." *The Marrow of Theology,* trans. by John D. Eusden, Pilgrim Press, 1968, p. 177. Ames was in the stream of English-Dutch Calvinism, and for years his text was used in American seminaries.

3. See *Melanchthon on Christian Doctrine*, ed. by Clyde L. Man-schreck, Oxford, 1965, p. 270. Melanchthon was the Lutheran who bridged the Reformation and Lutheran orthodoxy.

4. Ames, *op. cit.*, pp. 214, #5–9, and 216, #34.

5. See Donald McGavran, *Understanding Church Growth*, Eerdmans, 1970. A voluminous Church Growth literature has appeared of which this is a good example.

6. Howard Snyder, *The Community of the King*, Inter-Varsity Press, 1977, see pages 132ff. and *passim* for this and the following quotations.

7. See Orlando Costas, *The Church and Its Mission: A Shattering Critique from the Third World*, Tyndale, 1974. Costas has been quite critical of the Church Growth movement.

8. Karl Barth, "The Being of the Community," *Church Dogmatics*, IV, 1, T. & T. Clark, 1956, pp. 650ff.

9. Barth, "The Church—The Living Congregation of the Living Lord Jesus Christ," in *Man's Disorder and God's Design*, Harper, n.d., pp. 67ff.

10. Barth, *Church Dogmatics*, IV, 1, p. 652.

11. Barth, "The Church," *op. cit.*, p. 73.

12. Barth, "The Christian Community and the Civil Community," in *Community, State and Church*, Anchor, 1960, p. 153.

13. Barth, *Church Dogmatics*, IV, 1, p. 657.

14. Barth, *Church Dogmatics*, I, 1, T. & T. Clark, 1936, pp. 298–99.

15. Barth discusses the "true church" in volume IV, 2, T. & T. Clark, 1958, pp. 614ff. under the general topic of sanctification.

16. *Ibid.*, p. 620.

17. *Ibid.*, p. 621.

18. *Ibid.*, p. 618.

19. *Ibid.*, p. 627.

20. On the one hand he wrote, "We can never see the true Church as we can see a state in its citizens and officials and organs and laws and institutions. . . . What is visible in all this [members, officials, dogmatics, etc.] may be only a religious society." *Ibid.*, p. 619. However, in another setting he wrote that the church should be an example to the state in its organization; and he continued, "How can the world believe the gospel of the King and His Kingdom if by its own actions and attitudes the Church shows that it has no intention of basing its own internal policy on the gospel?" "The Christian Community and the Civil Community," p. 186. Barth's working image of the

church is institutional. He himself suggests the image of an inner circle gathered around Jesus Christ who is the common center of both church and state, but his working model remains the institution.

21. Colin Williams reports discussions of the role of the church in the world where this issue was already being debated in the early sixties. See *Where in the World?*, N.C.C., 1963, pp. 48f.; and *What in the World?*, N.C.C., 1964, pp. 42f. This line of discussion dominated at Bangkok (1973) with its theme of "Salvation Today," and at Nairobi (1975) with the theme "Jesus Christ Frees and Unites."

22. It is not at all clear in my mind that Barth and Bonhoeffer actually intended more than updated restatements of the positions of Luther and Calvin. Indeed, Bonhoeffer seems in some respects to have followed the pattern of Luther's own development although he developed the idea of the worldliness of the church much beyond Luther.

23. See *Report*, Section I, pp. 42–45.

24. Avery Dulles, *Models of the Church* (Doubleday, 1974), deals with the concept of church as sacrament in the Roman Catholic tradition. He is most helpful in some aspects, but again he virtually reduces the sacramental aspect to institutional structures and to the offices and rituals of the church. See pp. 58ff. and especially 63–64.

VII

AUTHENTIC COMMUNITY, A SIGN OF THE KINGDOM

Traditional protestant discussions of the life of the church in the world generally organized their material under the headings of "nature" and "mission." This very division of topics implies that while the two are related, the relation is not inherent. It suggests that the church in its essential form may exist apart from its evangelical mission. Emil Brunner's famous statement that "the church exists by mission like fire exists by burning" challenges this assumption, but the concept and the structures of the church based upon it linger on.

In this chapter we are raising the question of the *identity* and *role* of the church in the world.[1] These categories shift the older perspectives, usually considered under the categories of the nature and mission of the church. Nature and identity are related and overlapping, but they are not the same. The question about the nature of the church has to do with its essential (spiritual) constitution and institutional form, while identity has to do with authentic style and function. Similarly the emphasis on mission and role are not identical. Mission places emphasis on the goal, on activity and accomplishment. Role emphasizes the nature and value of involvement rather than the goal achieved.[2]

From this new vantage point, life and witness, method and message, nature and mission are seen to be one whole integrated experience. If we are concerned about the activity of the church, our concern is for "doing the truth." If we are interested in its essence or structure, it is in the reality of "the new creation." *The question about authentic witness is the question about the church's participation in the gospel of which it is the witnessing sign.* It simultaneously inquires into the communication and content of the gospel, expressed in the living form of the congregation. The life of the church *is* its witness. The witness of the church *is* its life. The question of authentic witness is the question of authentic community.

This concern for a community of communication is well illustrated in the work of the Waldensian leader Tullio Vinay. Following World War II he was the leader in forming a religious community in northern Italy called Agape. He and the community set about helping the Christian youth of the erstwhile warring nations of Europe to become reconciled and find anew their supranational identity in the Christian church. Then in 1961 he, along with part of the community at Agape, transferred to Riesi, Sicily, in a second attempt to give the gospel credible form in the midst of poverty and oppression. Writing about that experience ten years later he said:

> Our deepest motive in coming to Riesi may be summed up as follows: to incarnate the love (agape) of Christ among the disinherited, and to do this in and through the life and witness of a community or, if you like, of a community group. The temptation nowadays is to go to extremes: either to stick exclusively to verbal testimony (and no one, least of all the community, wants to underrate the importance of such testimony); or to throw oneself into social action with the assumption that the witness is implicit in such action. But neither of these ways is adequate. Words alone—even profound words—eventually just go over people's heads, like Sunday sermons in church. And social service and political action, without any explicit reference to the Gospel as their motive, fail to point to the Kingdom of God, even if one is fighting for the justice of that Kingdom.[3]

Vinay's interest in authentic community as a sign and witness to "the kingdom of God and his justice" (Matt. 6:33) points us to the identifying role of the church in our modern world. His is a vision of an open, healing community, demonstrating the "peace of God" and calling the world to be reconciled to God.

Images of Self-Identity

Vinay's image of the witnessing community is by no means the only operational self-image which is determining the life and witness of the church in the world. Indeed, there are a great variety of such images, many of which are neither consistent nor entirely unified, which influence the church's mode, style, and activity in the world. A glance at some of the more popular current ones for comparative purposes may be helpful.

I have chosen six images which seem to me to be fairly common among Protestants. (Roman Catholics will, I'm sure, recognize their own counterparts.) These first six are for contrast and comparison to the seventh, the image of healing community. They do not pretend to be complete, consistent models. In many cases more than one image is reflected in the stance and strategy of church groups. But the models do represent dominant self-images, and in most cases one image more than another influences group style and decision.

1. Evangelism, Inc.

The church is an organization to "save souls." The whole life of the congregation—preaching, Sunday School, prayer meetings, community canvassing, etc.—is geared toward evangelism. Crusades, rallies, tent meetings, Sunday morning radio and television broadcasts, etc., make up the major activities. Every sermon, including the Sunday morning sermon, is ended with an altar call for sinners.

The theology associated with this image teaches that salvation and the in-filling of the Spirit are for one purpose —more evangelism. The spiritual health of the congregation is diagnosed by assessing the number of new members that were won. And so it goes. The church is a corporation (non-profit, of course) for advertising and selling gospel.

2. Anti-Wickedness Campaign

The church is a voluntary religious society to uphold the cause of God against the devil, which usually means our "Christian" country against its enemies. Its slogan is "God and Country." Depending on the time and place, the enemy may be communism, liberalism, the demon alcohol, evolution, mongrelization of the race, or a nation with whom our country is at war.

The role of the church is to guard the spiritual treasures of the nation and to maintain righteousness because "righteousness exalteth a nation." It seeks to muster spiritual forces through prayer breakfasts, keeping prayer in the public schools, keeping Christians in sensitive political offices, and the like. The concern of the church and the culture overlap in the Christian family whose life is equally the basis for both.

3. Society for Spiritual Inspiration

The church is a sacramental center where individuals find inspiration and strength through the "means of grace"—word and sacramental signs—which the church dispenses. The Christian laypersons carry the burden of work in the world. In a gathered/scattered rhythm they shuttle back and forth between the "sacramental reality," where they receive spiritual inspiration, vision, and strength for the work, and the real world of action, where they spend most of their time and energy. We might say that the church provides religious "R and R" for battle-weary troops. Or, in a more sanctified manner of speaking, the church is the religious part of the world at prayer.

4. *Home, Sweet Home*

The church is the Christian's true home in the world. Here one is with God's family. Here in the fellowship of praise and prayer he/she finds the meaning and joy that makes life in the world tolerable, possibly even successful. The emphasis in this image is upon the church as a mystical, perhaps charismatic reality, where God's love is experienced in the fellowship of the saints. This sphere is where miracles are expected and experienced—a foretaste of heaven.

These last two models represent the spiritualization of the church in its Protestant churchly (no. 3) and sectarian (no. 4) forms. Indeed, the spiritualization of the church is so endemic to Protestantism that most people find it difficult to conceptualize a different way for the church to exist. The "real world" of activity and organization is the world of business, politics, education, and industry. The church is a spiritual fellowship, a *communio sanctorum* (communion of saints), rather than a socio-physical community with a visible historical existence. So entrenched and dominant is this model that even those evangelicals who are stressing "Church Growth" tend to make clear distinctions between the church as a non-institutional fellowship and the institutional "para-church" structures such as Sunday School, boards, agencies, denominational publishing companies, and Bible societies. Of course we must make distinctions between the congregation and specialized agencies, but both are social institutions within the visible community of the Spirit. Both have a "secular" reality and relevance to the witness.[4]

5. *The Separated Colony*

The church is a settlement of colonists who have been called out from the world. True Christians exist as a "third race." They must be separate from entangling alliances with the social and political institutions of the evil world. Therefore they form a parallel culture based upon the principles of the kingdom of God over against the world. The church is that visible community of Christian disciples separated unto God. In this way it attempts to bear witness to the world of God's covenant intention for all mankind.

One of the best examples of this model is the Society of Brothers. First formed in Germany in the 1920s, this group shares some of the self-understanding of the older Hutterite communities, yet is deeply concerned for the world and how to be a witness to the world. The community's life is strictly patterned after its understanding of Christ and his teaching; and although it shares freely of its material goods with the needy, its life is carefully separated from society around it.[5]

6. *The Revolutionary Invasion*

The church exists in the world as a liberation movement. It does not move "like a mighty army," but more like a revolutionary guerrilla band. Conscious of itself as part of the world, it takes the structures of the world very seriously. It works as an aggressive underground, propagandizing, making temporary alliances where expedient, supporting allied or friendly causes, and even joining in "liberating violence." What is significant and unique about it is its relation to Jesus and his goals for creating one new humanity. The Jesus liberators must always keep their own eschatological ends in view and work to move the historical process in that direction.

7. The Healing Community

The church is a community "in the world," but living by a different rule—the law of love. As Christ's representative it is a community of reconciliation, beseeching the world to be reconciled to God. Although it has a distinct life of its own, it is not closed or exclusive in membership. (Note the broken line.) This church is an entirely voluntary community open to whoever will be reconciled. Its goals are not for the exclusive advantage of its own members. It is "for the world" in that it seeks for the world what it seeks for itself, namely, *koinonia* in Christ. Living a life of *metanoia*, it symbolizes the lordship of Christ over the world, and calls that world to repent and accept his lordship.

The life of the healing community is characterized by and organized around its mission of reconciling witness. Evangelistic, that is, a community of witness to the evangel (good news), it defines evangelism as a holistic witness and not simply verbal proclamation. Its verbal witness is given integrity and power through the Holy Spirit's demonstration of justice, peace, and joy in its midst (Rom. 14:17, NEB).

161

John Perkins, founder of the community of witness called Voice of Calvary in Mendenhall and Jackson, Mississippi, discovered early in his experience of evangelistic preaching in the black community that in order to give the message integrity and power, he had to flesh out the gospel in ministries of social and political activity. Poverty, injustice, and exploitation had to be dealt with in the name of the gospel. Such ministries involved him and his congregation with both church members and non-church members alike. The witness was corporate and identifiable as the church making disciples, but its activities and its strategy thrust it into the world without sharply defined "churchly" and "parachurchly" organization and functions! Its evangelistic witness called individuals to faith and discipleship, and simultaneously challenged the demonic structures of racism which ruled both the secular and religious institutions of Mississippi.[6]

A Sign of the Kingdom

In order to focus our answer to the question, "How is the church in the world?" I propose two words, *sign* and *movement*. The church is in the world as a sign of the kingdom and part of the kingdom movement. In the rest of this chapter we shall consider the meaning and some of the implications of the authentic community as a sign of the kingdom. Then in the last chapter we will turn our attention to the church as the community and witness to the rule of God (a movement).

The simplest meaning of the word "sign" is token or indication. It may be an arbitrary signal or symbol, such as a whistle signaling the start of a game, or a letter ("w") indicating a particular sound. But we also use the word "sign" (arbitrary symbol) to mean an organically related indication, like smoke as a sign of fire. The latter is the sense intended here, as used by the apostle Paul, for example, when he writes to the Thessalonians that the greeting in his own handwriting is a "mark" or "sign" that the letter is truly from him (2 Thess. 3:17).

In the same way, the fourth Gospel uses the word *sē-meion*, translated as *sign*, to indicate the significance of Jesus' works of power. They give evidence of his identity. In 2:11, John refers to the sign as a manifestation of his "glory," that is, as a manifestation of his true character—his grace and truth. It marks him as the *authentēs*, the original master, the "Son of God."[7]

When we speak of the church as a sign of the kingdom, we point to it as a kind of evidence, an indicator which has an integral, organic relation to that other thing of which it is a sign. It participates in the reality to which it points. Only as such an authentic sign can the church be a credible witness.

The kingdom of God is the reality of which the church is a sign and to which it points. Jesus came to announce the inauguration of the kingdom, not the church. He taught that men should seek first the kingdom. And before he died he transferred the "keys of the kingdom" to his disciples, who were to become the apostolic foundation of the church. All this indicates that the church is penultimate to the kingdom, and acquires its identity and role in relation to the kingdom. What, then, is this kingdom?

The kingdom of God means simply the rule or government of God. The biblical concept is accurately summarized in the first three petitions of the Lord's Prayer, in which we pray for the coming of the kingdom. We pray:

> *Let your Name be held in respect,*
> *Let your Rule (Kingdom) come,*
> *Let your Will be done*
> *On earth as it is in heaven.*

This is a prayer that all mankind will come to acknowledge and live under God's covenant and enjoy his peace and security in true righteousness.

Jesus announced that he was inaugurating this rule. His disciples understood that his "powers" (miracles) were the tokens of it, and at the same time its inauguration. Matthew reports that when his opponents accused him of using the power of Satan, Jesus replied, "Every kingdom divided against itself is laid waste, . . . and if Satan casts out Satan, he is divided against himself. . . . But if it is by the Spirit of God that I cast out demons, then the kingdom of God has come upon you" (12:25–28). From this we can understand that where the power of God is manifested in overcoming sin and death, where the authority of God is respected under his covenant of life and peace, and where his justice is pursued in reconciliation and *koinonia*, there his rule is finding expression on earth.

To live under this rule is our salvation, for when Jesus becomes our Lord, then he is our savior. And we ask for this salvation for the whole world through Jesus, the *Lord*, when we pray, "Thy Kingdom come."

The church has always recognized that its identity is closely tied to its role as gatekeeper of this kingdom. When Jesus gave his disciples "the keys to the kingdom" (Matt. 16:18–19), he gave them the authority to open and shut its doors, that is, to let people into its blessings or to keep them out. Unfortunately the church soon began to interpret this as a legal authority handed on to the institutional church. What Jesus had in mind was something quite different. He was passing on his *kind of authority*. He was authenticating[8] their future ministry as his commissioned representatives. They were to be his original *ecclesia* (congregation)[9]—the authentic community which would continue as his "body" to perpetuate his presence and power.

As the authenticated congregation, this group, and those who would believe in Christ through their word (John 17:20), would be the continuing *sign* and witness to the presence of God's rule just as he himself had been.

Implications of the Word "Sign"

Several important implications of this way of speaking about the church should be noted. Although they are inferred in the term "sign of the kingdom," they clearly derive from Scripture also.

First, a sign is *not the final reality*. The church is not the kingdom, but points to it. Just as the messianic servant of Isaiah was given as a sign to the nations, so the messianic community continues to be that sign.[10] It points beyond itself to the kingdom of peace (shalom), the salvation of God yet to be fully revealed. The church is not the consummation of that which Jesus inaugurated, but rather his representative continuing his inaugural ministry, living in hope under the sign of the cross and the open tomb.

Second, a sign is *not an agent*. Much language of an earlier period has cast the church in the role of a managerial trustee. Images of *builder* (building the kingdom), *planter* (planting the church), *agent* (with an assignment demanding great courage and ingenuity), authoritative *manager* (vicar of Christ) are common parlance. We seem sometimes to have forgotten that God is the builder. And how is it that *planter* has accumulated a far more managerial nuance than *sower?* *Messengers* are agents, but the mission does not belong to the messenger. And household *servants*, even those who are made administrators, never define their own role and authority! In a culture which puts such great trust in technics and technique, social management, propaganda, and advertising, it becomes extremely easy to view the church as an agency which God has engaged to represent his cause in the world.

The mission is God's, not ours. His agent is the Holy Spirit, not the church. Only in a secondary sense may we speak of the church as agent of the Spirit. And even so, the metaphor of the body as the organ enlivened and controlled by the Spirit seems more appropriate. As Lesslie Newbigin so aptly put it:

> It [the Christian mission] is, so to say, not the motor but the blade, not the driving force but the cutting edge. . . . They [Christians] go through history as the witness people, in whom the Spirit is present to bear witness to the real meaning of things which happen in the world, so that—*in relation to these things*—men are compelled to make decisions for or against God. . . . They [the acts of Christians in service] will be signs rather than instruments. . . . They are not the *means* by which God establishes his Kingdom. They are witness to its present reality.[11]

Third, a sign *must be credible*, to function as a sign. In spite of the incessant talk about the necessity of the church's witness being relevant, it appears that the more serious problem is *credibility*. Years ago P. T. Forsyth lamented "a church whose power is not equal to its claim."[12] More recently one of the study sections of the World Council of Churches meeting in Uppsala (1968) observed, "The words of proclamation are doubted when the church's own life fails to embody the marks of the new humanity."[13]

Historically, Protestant orthodoxy and its theological heirs, fundamentalism and evangelicalism, have not been overly concerned with the question of authentic community because the sign of the kingdom was identified with the written word and not with the witnessing church. The concern was for a correct word. Thus, in this tradition, great theological importance has been attached to theories of *verbal* inspiration and orthodox *statements*. The church's responsibility has been understood as preaching a correct message which is *self-authenticating*. The persuasiveness of the message has had little to do with the credibility of the church's life and witness. Rather, it depended upon the election or predestination of God on the one hand, and the inner witness of the Holy Spirit on the other.

We have examined the relation of church and Scripture in Chapter 3, but here we must note further the subtle transformation which occurs when the sign is identified with words, whose credibility is based upon a *self*-authenticating process of inspiration. This kind of theology takes the primary focus off Jesus Christ as the authenticating reality. The credibility of the sign does not rest on its Christly authenticity, that is, its participation in the original authoritative reality, but upon a process which supposedly gives it a self-authenticating character. This, in effect, moves the question of credibility from a living historical ground to a rational one. Further, by the same token, it takes the focus off the living church as a continuing witness to the kingdom, and places it upon the words of Scripture.

The church must in essence, as a sign of the rule of God, express in its own life the presence and power of that rule. "Sign" means authentic expression of the reality to which it points. The question here is not the perfection of the church (or of the individual) as a witness. As we noted, a sign is not the fulfillment. Of course, "we see in a mirror dimly" (1 Cor. 13:12).

Rather, it is a matter of the authority of the church in its proclamation of the gospel. As P. T. Forsyth said, "In so far as the Church is expressive of that Gospel, and created by it, it shares in its authority. But only as the Gospel's new creation and moral organ . . . ; only in the evangelical sense in which it is created . . . by the Gospel, as the experient trustee of the saving word, as its offspring and organ."[14] When the church contradicts its own proclamation by accommodating to the old order, it contradicts its credibility and the authority of the message it proclaims. The hallmark of authenticity is *metanoia,* and that mark gives credibility to the church's proclamation of the lordship of Christ.

Real Signs

Do such signs of the kingdom exist among us, or are we merely talking about an ideal type of which existing churches are at best only poor approximations? Before we answer that question we must remember that we are not asking for perfect specimens, "holy clubs," or super-human religious models. We are asking whether there exist congregations and communities of disciples who, with integrity, are taking seriously the life-style of Jesus, forming relationships patterned on *koinonia,* bearing authentic witness to the incarnation of God's love and salvation. The answer to that question is yes, there are these signs among us. No single community furnishes *the* model for authenticity. Nevertheless, examples of Christian groups who have heard the call to corporate witness as the body of Christ may be found around the world.

There are, in fact, many Christian congregations, house churches, *koinonia* groups, mission fellowship groups, charismatic fellowships, as well as communally organized extended households and larger intentional communities, which have caught the vision of a holistic, corporate witness. All of these may be subsumed under the classification of

Christian communities. They seek to embody in their own life and fellowship the good news of the kingdom. They indeed signal the new community. We can in the following pages refer to only a few of those that are perhaps pioneers in this new movement of the Spirit.

The Christian ashrams of India, in which believers form as communities of worship, church renewal, and service, come immediately to mind. These communities of witness gather all of life into a holistic pattern of Christian discipleship. Ashram life finds its focus in the community discipline of worship and dependence on God. Its reason for existence, however, it not an ascetic discipline of a higher level of obedience to Christ. Rather, its corporate goal is witness to the new creation through proclamation, service, and worship. The community identifies with the sin and need of the world in a life of *metanoia*, which expresses itself in a simple living standard characteristic of the poorer classes, mutual sharing, and in dedication to a life of service for the world. Its very life, as well as its verbal witness, is centered in a covenant of *shalom* and calls men and women to wholeness in Christ. Such ashram communities are kingdom centers seeking to live now under the lordship of Christ and to continue his redemptive ministry.

In America, Koinonia Farm, first organized by Clarence Jordan and his associates, has been another sign. In this community, "the kingdom of God and his justice" is the prime concern. In order not to cut itself off from the organized churches, the community was explicitly formed not as a "church," although worship and study of Scripture have been an integral part of its life, but as an authentic witness to the message and style of Jesus. In the midst of economic competition and exploitation, this community of the King was organized as a *koinonia*. In the heartland of racially segregated Georgia, the community has been aggressively open to all people, even at the cost of persecution. In the name of Jesus and under his explicit lordship, the community has identified with the disadvantaged and seeks the welfare of the most needy. It offers an evangelical witness to the new possibility of wholeness in Christ.

The story of the charismatic renewal and reorganization of the Church of the Redeemer in Houston, Texas, provides another exciting example of a congregation seeking and finding an authentic, corporate, Christly life-style. This congregation was literally reborn as a cluster of house fellowships open to the alienated and despairing people of one of our major cities. Ministries of various kinds have formed out of the community of worship and nurturing fellowship, calling people to new fullness of life in Christ. It has become in truth a healing community of Christian disciples.

We have referred to other communities such as Voice of Calvary, Agape in Italy, and Church of the Savior at other places in the discussion. All of these provide further examples of kingdom signs among us. One more community which has recently made a significant impact on the American scene is the Sojourners, located in Washington D.C. This group of younger people from strict fundamentalist backgrounds dared, like Clarence Jordan a generation before them, to ask what radical obedience to the New Testament might look like. They struggled with their inherited individualism, affluence, and pietistic religion as they learned what life together in Christ means.

Their community is organized as a communal fellowship attempting to demonstrate in their own life-style the reorientation toward God which is the authenticating hallmark of witness. Located in the inner city, its households have made it their primary responsibility to share their new life together in Christ with their immediate neighbors. Theirs is a ministry of reconciliation and community building, which, as they point out, is the most radical of all political activity. They live as a sign of the new possibility of life together in Christ, offering a prophetic challenge to the institutionalized churches, the government, and society at large through their publication, also named *Sojourners*.

Each of these communities has its own personality, style, and emphasis. But each, as a visible manifestation of the body of Christ, offers a distinct alternative to the alienation and brokenness of sinful human society. Each offers the individual new personal wholeness in the body of Christ.

Each stands as a sign of the new creation challenging more conventional Christianity, as well as secular society, to recognize the new covenant offered in Christ as the pattern of authentic human community.

Notes to Chapter VII

1. I have borrowed these designations—identity and role—from William Glasser's *The Identity Society*, Harper & Row, 1972. Glasser's thesis is that in the 1950s, the western third of the world's population began to notice the emergence of a new cultural era which he calls a "civilized identity society." In contrast to the old "survival society," which was security and goal oriented, now identity and role as loved and worthy human beings has become the dominant concern. His insight can help us see more clearly the direction of the quest for an authentic expression of community.

2. Two books which might illustrate this difference are Donald Miller's *The Nature and Mission of the Church* (1957), and a recent book by Avery Dulles, *Models of the Church* (1974), although Miller more than many previous theologians recognizes the necessity for an essential integration.

3. Tullio Vinay, " 'Servizio Cristiano' in Riesi, Sicily," *International Review of Missions* (Jan., 1973), p. 66.

4. See Howard Snyder, *The Community of the King*, Inter-Varsity Press, 1977, pp. 158ff.; and the works of Ralph Winter upon whom he depends for this kind of analysis, especially "The Two Structures of God's Redemptive Mission," *Missiology*, 2:1 (Jan., 1974), pp. 121–39.

5. See Benjamin Zablocki, *The Joyful Community*, Penguin Books, 1971; and the writings of Eberhard and Emmy Arnold, published by Plough Publishers.

6. Perkins tells his story in *A Quiet Revolution: The Christian Response to Human Need*, Word Books, 1976.

7. Thus it becomes more apparent why Jesus refused to do "wonders" (what are popularly called miracles today) on demand in order to impress the crowds. Such wonders unavoidably would have had the character of arbitrary symbols because they are not set in the context of discerning response.

8. The first definition of authenticate in the *Oxford English Dictionary* is "to invest (a thing) with authority."

9. The New Testament word, translated church, is *ekklēsia.* Unfortunately we have no one word in English to translate *ekklēsia.* It literally means an assembly gathered by a call. It parallels the word "synagogue," which means to come together. The word "church" stems from the Greek *kuriakon.* (Cf. the German *Kirche,* and the Scottish *Kirk.*) *Kuriakon* means "of the lord" or "house of the lord." However, church has come to mean a quite distinct religious institution in western society. In order, therefore, to get back to the original meaning I have used "congregation." Although this may indicate for many simply a Sunday morning gathering for worship, I wish to include its whole group life. Compare the German *Gemeinde,* which emphasizes the community as a gathered fellowship.

10. The terms in Isaiah are "witness," "light," and "covenant." See 42:6; 43:10; 49:6, 8. Whether the servant is Israel, messiah, or the messianic community, and it is most likely to be understood as all three of these, the meaning is clearly the same.

11. Lesslie Newbigin, *Trinitarian Faith and Today's Mission,* John Knox Press, 1964, pp. 37–38, 43. Newbigin's book, first published in 1963, anticipated much of the ecumenical discussion about the church as sign. That discussion tended, even more than Newbigin himself, to view the sacramental life of the church as an interpretative sign indicating the inner meaning of what was happening in the world. The real focus of interest was upon what God is doing in the world for politics and culture. The church was viewed as an ancillary function to that action.

12. P. T. Forsyth, *The Principle of Authority,* Independent Press, 1952, p. 322.

13. *The Uppsala Report 1968,* Official Report of the Fourth Assembly of the World Council of Churches, ed. by Norman Goodall, Geneva, 1968, p. 32.

14. Forsyth, *op. cit.,* pp. 325–26.

VIII

COMMUNITY AS AUTHENTIC WITNESS

M. M. THOMAS, CHURCH LEADER FROM SOUTH IN-
dia, has observed that, "The Kingdom of God is a most difficult Biblical theme. Most of the theological debates centre
around the way in which we understand it. Proclaiming the
Kingdom, witnessing to the Kingdom, extending the Kingdom, building the Kingdom, realising the Kingdom, waiting
for the Kingdom, experiencing the Kingdom within—all
these are based on different ways of understanding the Kingdom of God."[1]

The differences and difficulties in understanding the
kingdom are reflected also in the differences in understanding the meaning and form of witness to Jesus Christ in our
age. "Winning souls for Jesus," saving souls from hell, con-
verting individuals to Jesus, making persons whole,
humanizing or making life whole, preaching Jesus Christ as
savior, preaching "new birth," making disciples, showing the
love of Jesus, preaching *shalom* (peace)—all these, while not
mutually exclusive, do call for different approaches and
strategies!

In the current discussion of these questions the issues
are joined between the voices of evangelicalism, represented
at the International Congress on World Evangelism at
Lausanne (1974), and the voices of the Commission on
World Mission and Evangelism of the World Council of

Churches heard at Uppsala (1968), Bangkok (1973), and Nairobi (1975). Each of these ecumenical discussions contains a spectrum of opinion in itself, but they also represent two distinct theological traditions within Protestantism. Terminology, meanings, and special emphases have grown out of a history of conversation and debate. Indeed, understanding the loyalties, emotional responses, and critical judgments that emerge is often difficult if one cannot identify the positions being represented. While all speak of salvation, peace, and the kingdom of God, the meanings are obviously varied. From whence stems the conflicting diversity in the witness to salvation?

The Witness to Salvation

Like every individual, evangelicalism has many ancestors, all of whom have contributed to its genetic pool. But the grandparents who gave birth to one of its parents, fundamentalism, were revivalism and Plymouth Brethrenism. The genes of this parent have remained dominant in the formation of its concepts of witness. From these precursors it has inherited its strong emphasis on witness as evangelistic preaching (words), and on salvation as the spiritual transaction of justification.[2]

Speakers in the Bible and Prophetic Conferences of the 1870s and 80s idealized the preacher with the open Bible as the model for witness. Some said that no one deserved to hear the message twice until everyone had had the opportunity of hearing it once, in reaction against an older strategy of "Christianizing" a small area of culture from which it was hoped that the mission would spread. (This latter view was often caricatured as trying to catch all the fish in one small pond before going to the great oceans where untold millions of fish waited to be caught.)

The individual to be saved was viewed as "a soul to be snatched from the burning." Salvation as justification was, to put it bluntly, a negotiation within the Godhead in which Jesus made satisfaction to the Father for man's sin. Each individual soul was released from its deserved punishment by belief in Jesus' work of atonement. All this had to do with the individual's interior spiritual relation to God.

Salvation was not understood as a relation in community under the covenant of Christ. Souls were called out from the old natural ("fallen") community, but not really into a viable new one. They were simply told to go back into their natural communities of family and vocation to live as new individuals. "Church" was organized as an association of believing individuals for specified purposes—more a corporation than a community in form.

The teachers in the Prophetic and Bible Conference movement, and those who followed them, practically ignored the community aspects of salvation, partly because of their extreme pessimism about the depravity of human nature and society. Community, according to their view, would be given in the future millennial kingdom for which the saved were to wait. The only present community was that fostered by togetherness in the waiting room.

Meanwhile the older pattern and understanding of the church and its mission continued at home and on foreign compounds. This older strategy attempted to develop new *Christian* cultural communities by building a Christian institution. In America it was assumed that the church had the responsibility to influence and guide the social order toward more Christian expressions by forming organizations for educational, medical, social, and moral reform alongside the institutional church. (The idea that the church's mission was to "Christianize" civilization was much older than the Social Gospel.) In foreign "non-Christian cultures," missionaries promoted many social causes such as orphanages, hospitals, and schools as part of the Christian witness. It was argued that sick bodies and illiterate minds were poor candidates for the gospel. The Christian faith was viewed as a powerful force for moral uplift and civilization. Where the theological rationale for this venture was self-consciously postmillennial, men talked of spreading the kingdom of God and viewed the new Christian cultural enclaves as extensions of it.

Even so, the explicit end of such mission was not life in covenant community, but simply a matter of following inherited patterns of western Christianity, which had integrated the religious and civic communities, and of adapting them to the new situations. Indeed, especially on "foreign mission" locations, so long as the missionary compound remained physically and culturally separated from the native church, any real possibility for Christian community was effectively thwarted. Where Christian communities emerged in such forms as castes, villages, or attachment to western institutions (the "compound"), it was largely a result of reaction and counter pressure by the indigenous community which attempted to seal off the new cultural invader.

In the early 1900s, proponents of a more humanistic version of the Social Gospel attempted to recreate the secular social community as a means of saving the individuals who were conditioned by it. This understanding of Christian witness was much influenced by the new sociological recognition that social and economic factors play a significant part in forming the individual character and self-image. Thus, the argument ran, if Christians will work to Christianize the political and economic structures, they can create conditions that will foster the conversion of individuals. Christianizing the social order was equated with building the kingdom of God!

The Impact of Bonhoeffer

As seen in the last chapter, the more recent debate in ecumenical Protestant circles has been greatly influenced by the concepts of men like Barth and Bonhoeffer. Barth, of course, led the way, but in the more recent discussion Bonhoeffer has had a formative influence.

Our purpose is not to trace Bonhoeffer's own development in detail, but rather to glean some insight into the current discussion about the identity and role of the church in the world. However, his own pilgrimage is important because both his example and theology have had a significant impact. He has furnished many of the theological idioms such as the church "taking its agenda from the world," being "a part of the world" and "for the world," or "humanization" as the historical goal of the kingdom. He has been a germinal influence in "liberation theology," and continues to point the direction for much conceptualization and strategy.

Barth reacted strongly against the naturalistic assumptions of liberalism's Social Gospel, and he insisted that the church can never "build the kingdom." He did not, of course, view the kingdom as a future millennial possibility, although he did view it as a fulfillment of God's purposes for history. In his terminology, the "sanctification of all humanity" is God's goal for history, and both in our present experience and in the consummation of cosmic history, sanctification is totally God's act, received as a gift "by faith" like justification. The church can only bear witness to the work of God by faithfully preaching the Bible.

Bonhoeffer, at least in his earlier writings, put more stress on the visible characteristics of the church. "The Body of Christ," he wrote, "takes up space on earth," being a social reality and not just a religious experience or idea. And as a visible body, it "claims a space of its own" in the world.[3] The question, then, is what kind of "space" does it need? How is it in the world—as a religious institution? a spiritual fellowship? a small group formed on face-to-face relationships? an organized worshiping congregation? a social-spiritual mission of disciples? an organized effort for evangelism?

A closer look at Bonhoeffer's concept of the church in and for the world will help us to see the shape of the issue, and in order to understand his answer to the above questions we must first observe how he conceptualizes human relationships and responsibility in society.

Following the classical Lutheran pattern of analysis, he held that there are four social orders which define the spheres of responsibility for each individual. These are "labour, culture, marriage and the family, government, and the Church."[4] He preferred the word "mandate" to "order" because it "refers more clearly to a divinely imposed task" than to a static order of being. Every person must live and operate simultaneously in relation to all four mandates. Each of these divine mandates given in and through Jesus Christ defines a specific sphere of responsibility, and God's intended order in Christ is realized only when they operate in the proper complementarity and tension. The church has its own specific mandate from Christ, namely, to proclaim Jesus Christ as the Lord of the entire world of men and things.

The first three mandates in effect define "the world." But the church must find "space" in that world. It exists only as "part of the world," he said, not separate from it. And yet it has a peculiar and different kind of existence in the world, being "for the world." In a sense not true of the others, it has a transient and instrumental character. It exists as a "self-contained community" with its own mandate—not as an end in itself, but as "merely a means to an end."

If such an analysis seems abstract, it may help to point out that it is merely the theological rationale for the common Protestant pattern of church organization and life in the secular order. Life in the world can be described in terms of fairly concrete social, economic, and political activities, and individual Christians fulfill their vocations by participation in these activities. The church in public worship also is an empirical religious activity, but beyond that its role and influence in and for the world is described in abstract and spiritualized terms. The church as a visible society, a congregation of saints, with a mandate which can be described in a pattern of social relationships and observable actions, impinging on the world of politics and economics, has been consistently rejected as theologically inconsistent with the Protestant principle of justification by faith. Even Bonhoeffer, who in his earlier years experimented with a religious community of students and teachers and claimed a "space in the world" for the community, ended by spiritualizing and individualizing that space.

Bonhoeffer's first answer to the question, "How is the church in the world?" is that it is in the world as a "mandate." It exists as a task rather than an institution, a relationship rather than an organization, an action rather than a structure. This kind of imagery led Colin Williams to phrase the question, "Where in the world is the church?" And the answer to that question according to Bonhoeffer is that *it is where the mandate is being carried out*. Where the proclamation of Jesus Christ as lord of the world is being preached, believed, and obeyed.

But the question persists. What visible form does this proclamation take? Is it essentially a spoken word which exists only in the act of speaking and hearing? And perpetuated in the constant repetition of preaching and response? Bonhoeffer is inclined toward this Lutheran bias. Or is it a written word which has an existence and dynamic of its own which forms the space for a continuing theological tradition? This is the bias of Reformed orthodoxy. Or is it embodied in a community of witness which has visible continuity as a community? And if so, how does that community relate to the other social orders with their mandates?

According to Bonhoeffer, the church has its existence—its "space"—in the world in two distinct forms. First, it is visible as the *congregation (Gemeinde)*. In this form it is "primarily a baptismal and eucharistic congregation and only secondarily a preaching congregation."[5] It becomes visible in these activities and in the "offices" or "ministries" associated with its sacramental life. Second, the church is visible in the lives of *its individual members in the world*. "The Church," he wrote, "needs space not only for her liturgy and order, but also for the daily life of her members in the world. That is why we must now speak of the living-space (*Lebensraum*) of the visible Church."[6]

First, then, the church as congregation is visible as a "self-contained community."[7] He is careful to say on this point, however, that true Christian community is not to be *equated* with the human religious community. With calculated precision he delimited the basis and scope of fellowship in Christian community. It is not based on desire or need for human fellowship, on familial or cultural preferences, on friendship or emotional attachment. Neither is it maintained by the experience of immediate ("primary") relationships of any kind, nor by camaraderie in moral or religious causes. It is a "purely spiritual fellowship." He wrote:

> Christianity means community through Jesus Christ and in Jesus Christ. . . . Not what a man is in himself as a Christian, his spirituality and piety, constitutes the basis of our commu-

nity. What determines our brotherhood is what that man is by reason of Christ. Our community with one another consists solely in what Christ has done to both of us.[8]

This spiritual community is most purely and powerfully expressed in the "uncorrupted ministry of Word and sacraments." In these expressions of its fellowship in Christ, the community fulfills its mandate and makes its proclamation to the world.

Although the community has a life of its own, this life is not a *life for itself*. Like its Master, it too is "for the world." Indeed, the community becomes the body of Christ precisely and only if it is "for the world" in its essential character and life. "If the congregation fails to fulfil this responsibility it ceases to be the congregation of Christ."[9] Or, as he put it in another passage, "The Church as a self-contained community serves to fulfil the divine mandate of proclamation . . . which means that the congregation itself is merely an instrument, merely a means to an end." Only as the church understands itself as servant and is *"adapted to the purpose of the world"* can the congregation become "the center of all God's dealing with the world."[10]

Two other crucial qualifications of the community are implied or stated obliquely if not explicitly. The spiritual community does not exist as a full-blown social community, but within limits defined by a specialized mandate. It does not attempt to duplicate the mandates of the family, labor, or government, for example, to set up "Christian businesses," or organize "Christian political parties."[11] Nor does it try to be the religious counterpart of the secular world—a society alongside and parallel to the secular community. It rather is simply a part of the world—that part which already recognized the lordship of Christ and sacramentally stands before God as "deputy" for the world.[12]

It follows that the congregation, or spiritual community, does not attempt to offer the world a superior moral or religious example. Precisely speaking, it can properly become an example only in faithfully carrying out its own particular mandate, which is to call the world to live under Christ's dominion. In this way it sets an example of proper submission to the lordship of Christ. Under no circumstances should "the 'law' of the Church as a community" become "the law of the worldly order." The church should not try to "Christianize" the world by patterning it after its own religious and moral model, but rather should seek to reconcile it to Christ, to free it to be "genuinely and completely worldly," which means liberate it to "realize its own essential character which has its foundation in Christ."

Apparently Bonhoeffer's earlier hopeful vision of the church as a visible community changed as the rise of Hitler and the war brought German Christians to an ever deepening crisis in the 1940s. Whether his probing of the implications of a "non-religious interpretation of Christ" and what it means to be a Christian was merely an attempt to understand what he felt he must do, or whether his theological rationale led to his action, is immaterial to our point. In any case, in his letters from prison he shifted his emphasis to such an extent that at one point his friend Bethge wrote him asking whether he thought there was "any 'room' left for the Church, or whether that room had gone for good."[13]

Bethge describes the shift as away from a quest for Christ's presence in a visible community of discipleship in the world, to the presence of Christ in the world in the form of individual "ethical responsibility for the concrete guilt-covered world." For Bonhoeffer himself this meant re-evaluating his own convictions about Christian pacificism and his official position in the Confessing Church, and involving himself in a conspiracy to overthrow Hitler's government by assassinating Hitler himself. "Finally, in 1944," writes Bethge, "the presence of Christ [for Bonhoeffer] is found in the conformation of man with Christ's messianic suffering, risking a 'church' which allows itself to be *drawn anonymously into the world.*"[14]

Summary and Critique

In spite of the emphasis upon Christian community in Bonhoeffer's writings, the greatest share of responsibility for the church's visible witness in the world falls on the individual Christian in his secular vocation, in the familiar Protestant pattern. The mandate given to the church impinges upon the life of the world precisely in the vocation of each individual Christian.[15] He or she is to remain in the world fully subject to the authority of its mandates given by Christ—in labor, family, and government. These mandates, according to Bonhoeffer, are not derived from a "natural law" or "created order" outside of Christ. Therefore Christians' "worldliness does not divide them from Christ."[16]

Christians live in the world as members of the body of Christ. As new creatures they bear witness that Jesus Christ is the foundation of the secular order. But this does not mean that they should exhibit a special religious piety or morality, nor that they are personal evangelists recruiting new church members. Neither does it mean that they are trying in puritan fashion to bring the world under the religious discipline of the church. Rather, they are in the world to serve the world, and to testify that Jesus Christ is in fact the foundation of the world's own authentic reality. "The Church must share in the secular problems of ordinary human life, not dominating, but helping and serving."[17] This is what he meant by the *non-religious* shape of the church in the world.

But Bonhoeffer was not a secularist. "It is, of course, to be assumed," he wrote, "that this testimony before the world can be delivered in the right ways only if it springs from a hallowed life in the congregation of God."[18] He also wrote of this spiritual dimension of the Christian's life in the world as the "secret discipline." He considered it absolutely necessary for the Christian, but, presumably, to recommend it to the world would have smacked of religion.

And so, with a certain reluctance and disappointment, we conclude that the promising insights of the *Communion of Saints* (1927) and *The Cost of Discipleship* (1931) were finally laid aside.[19] Along with Luther, whom he greatly admired and with whom he closely identified, he rejected first the possibility and later the advisability of gathering an authentic visible community as a sign in the world. In its place he established the "secret discipline," and the hallowed fellowship of the spiritual communion of saints which becomes visible in the *proclamation* (sacraments and preaching) of the lordship of Christ over the world. Community as a social reality may be found only within the orders of the world, and there only at elusive moments and in fragments as a gift of the Holy Spirit to faith.

A Parabolic Interlude

In the light of this historical background, how shall we understand the church's witness? How is it related to God's cosmic purposes which we believe were set forth in Christ? How can the community be a witness to the kingdom of God? Perhaps instead of continuing the theoretical language, a parable can help us to conceptualize the relationships.

The rule of God is like an underground river flowing from its source high in the glaciers toward its eventual destination. Depending on the terrain, it sometimes surfaces in a quiet pool in the desert to create an oasis. Again it emerges as springs and rivulets of "still waters." And then when spring thaws melt the snows, the streams become a surging torrent, clearing old clogged channels and creating new ones for the river. Finally the great river below the ground, and the surface estuaries, having made their way through the rich delta country, merge in the ocean.

Always the great river is there to be tapped by wells deep into the earth. Sometimes it gushes out under artesian pressure, and sometimes it lies cool and deep, to be reached only by disciplined human effort. But wherever it comes to the surface, it brings life and activity. People and animals flock to it for refreshment and cleansing.

Just so "the river of life" flowing from the throne of God (Rev. 22:1ff.) flows through the terrain of history until it emerges finally in the midst of the city of God, bringing life and healing to the nations.

Certainly this river flowing from the *throne* of God suggests his beneficent rule or kingdom. With similar imagery, but making a slightly different point, the prophet Ezekiel saw a vision of the river issuing from the temple of God as a small stream of fresh water that grew broader and deeper. Along its banks were abundant life and well-being. And where it entered "the stagnant waters of the sea, the waters [became] fresh" (Ezek. 47; esp. vv. 6–12).

Like all metaphors, of course, this one of the underground river has its limitations. But it can help us visualize the relation of the rule of God and its many manifestations among us throughout history. The rule of God has found expression in the spiritual depths of individuals in whose innermost being it has become "a well of living waters." It has surfaced in groups like monastic communities that preserved and kept available the wells dug by the ancients. It emerged like springs of refreshment and renewal in men and movements like those of St. Francis and Peter Waldo. At other times it has broken free in a great movement of spiritual power, bringing reformation and change.

Never has its source been identified solely with the church, or its influence confined to the church. Never has the rule of God been contained in its visible expressions. But time and again the visible church has been the place, the terrain, where the fresh, life-giving waters have broken to the surface. And always where the rule has become manifest in history it has brought new life and created community and well-being. Authentic community has always been the witness to its presence.

The Jesus Community

The continuing witness of Jesus, the *Christ,* exists in the world as the messianic community. In Scripture it is referred to as the "body of Christ" which is enlivened by his Spirit. This body is in the world as he was in the world.

In popular lingo, the messianic community has been dubbed the "Jesus community" ("people" or "family"). While often meaning less than I intend by messianic community, this language is an excellent designation if we keep clearly in mind that Jesus came as the Messiah, that is, the Christ. Calling it the "Jesus community" gives it a concrete historical reference, tying it to his authenticating character and example. As Jesus himself bore witness to the kingdom of God, so the community continues to bear its witness. Authentic witness is messianic in form and purpose.

Several important implications follow from this New Testament concept. First, the messianic community is the *community under the Messiah's (Christ's) commission.* The church is the *servant of Jesus Christ* for the world.

Bonhoeffer's insistence that the church is "for the world" is true and a needed corrective. "God so loved the world," wrote John (3:16). Jesus gave his life for the world, not only for the church as some of the orthodox Reformed theologians of the seventeenth century held. The church as a religious institution is not an end in itself, but is expendable in the service of Christ.

All this is well taken. But a number of contemporary theologians under the influence of Bonhoeffer have extended the servant image of the church, speaking of it as *"servant of the world."*[20] The church's ministry, they argue, must take place in the secular institutions of politics, commerce, and the like. It must be shaped according to the needs and for the proper ends of these institutions, and must "take its agenda from the world."

Such a position begins with the conception of "the church" as a religious institution among the other institutions of society. It argues that the church's relevance in the modern world is in direct proportion to its ability to give a "lay" secular witness, not as a community, but as scattered individuals living and working incognito in the world.

In reply, it may be pointed out, in the first place, that the community itself, of which the great institutional structures are often little more than a desiccated shell, exists as witness of the rule of God. The *koinonia* of the first Christians in Jerusalem living out their commitment to the Christ in the new community was what caught the attention of the spectators. And so it continued during those first centuries. In the second place, while the *sphere* of the community's service is the world, and while the *recipient* of its witness is the world, the *director of services* is the Christ. The church serves the world under the apostolic commission of the Christ, not second to the world for the world's programs and purposes.

The community has been formed and deputized, as it were, to carry on the messianic mission. That is why it exists, and the mission gives it its form. A number of Christian communities have caught this vision of the centrality of mission in the life of the church, and have attempted to give it expression in the organization and life of the congregation. Perhaps none has worked at it more deliberately over an extended period of time than the Church of the Savior in Washington, D.C.

In her latest book, *The New Community*, Elizabeth O'Connor, a member of the community, makes the point quite emphatically that no community can truly participate in Christ unless it acts as an open, servant community identifying with the most needy of the world. Taking this with the greatest seriousness, the original congregation of Church of the Savior, which supported members in a number of separate missions, reconstituted itself into several sister communities, each organized around specific missions. The group's life of worship and individual spiritual discipline aimed at full integration into, and expressed identification with, Christly service to the needy. Nor is service defined simply as a social service project, but as a liberating, healing ministry to bring individuals to wholeness in Christian community.

The "missionary mandate" is not a religious *project* of the church to be assigned to a department or board, and fulfilled by individuals who go as "missionaries." Neither is it an altruistic gesture in which the community shares some of the blessings which Christ has bestowed upon it. The mission is not the largess of the church. The mandate forms the community and gives it coherence. The unity of the church (catholicity) is found in the service of Christ. Only as it loses itself in the quest for the "kingdom of God and his righteousness" will it be given its authentic life.

The community's purpose and methods, its choice of priorities, its style—all are determined by the messianic mandate. We must be cautious of a language that calls for the church to take its "agenda" and "structures" from the world in order to be relevant for the world, for the world cannot be saved on its own terms. There must be *metanoia*.

Second, the community *continues the basic stance of Christ's ministry and mission*. Its fundamental character and purpose are not different from the ministry of Jesus.

Jesus came to inaugurate, that is, to announce and begin a movement. He did not bring the rule of God to completion, not even in his resurrection, but promised to return and complete what he had begun. In the meantime he left a community of anticipation and witness to continue his introductory ministry.

What Jesus did as the initiator of the new movement could only be done by him, and he did it "once for all." The mission of the messianic community is possible only because of what he did; it grows out of his ministry and follows it in time, remaining dependent upon him as *authentēs*. In this sense the community's ministry is not the repetition of his ministry. Clearly stated, *the messianic community is the continuation of his introductory ministry*. It continues to "share in his suffering, becoming like him in his death" (Phil. 3:10). It does not supersede his ministry or substitute for it. The kingdom of God is yet in an initiatory stage, and neither in realization nor in abeyance. The church still prays, "Thy kingdom come . . . on earth as it is in heaven."

Since the kingdom remains incipient, its manifestation in the messianic community is *anticipatory*.[21] The community has received the Holy Spirit as the "first fruits," or "witness," of the new reality, enabling it to continue the anticipatory presence of the rule of God. In the parable of the pounds, for example, the community is likened to a household of servants who have been entrusted to invest the master's wealth for him while he is gone on a trip to "receive a kingdom" (Lu. 19:11–27). These servants are already part of his household under his dominion, and their custodial activity anticipates his new status and their own participation in it.

In this sense we may say that the community remains "a part of the world"—that part of the world which already accepts and lives under the lordship of Christ for its own and the world's salvation. It knows the struggle, imperfection, and pain of the world, and continues to be a participant in the socio-political order. The question is *how* it participates, not whether it should participate. The community is caught in the ambiguities and confusion of this age, yet lives "in hope." But in the world as that new historical reality which came to being in Christ, it exists where men and women who are conformed to the image of Christ know God as father and seek to live together under his covenant in repentance and submission.[22]

Because the authentic community is a renewed "part of the world," it should not be understood as a universal, idealistic model that is supracultural—a rational principle or moral ideal. Neither should it be viewed as a "colony of heaven" living in separated "perfection." Attempts to incorporate this model have always demonstrated that even if one can take the community out of the world, one cannot take the world out of the community.

The authentic community, rather, continues to exist in a pluralistic, unredeemed world as a redemptive possibility within and for human cultures.[23] It begins with the given in the indigenous situation, and brings the criterion of Christ's authenticity to test its human validity. Remember in this connection that the biblical definition of human is "to be conformed to the image of his Son," who is the "image of God." In the formation of its own life as part of the world, therefore, the community calls for *metanoia* and conformity to Christ for the sake of the world.

The model for this, of course, is Jesus himself. His life was a thoroughly integrated, indigenous cultural expression of the "Word." He came not only as man in a generic sense, but embodied as a Jewish male. That, as we have seen, is incarnation. Thus the church must embody the love of Christ in any contextual form in which it finds itself, and bear a contextual witness to his lordship and mission.

The Open Community

Third, the messianic community *shares Christ's openness to the world.* Again, Jesus himself is the original or prototype of openness. He showed an amazing, and to the religious folk of his day offensive, freedom in his association with "sinners." No religious prudery or clerical snobbishness closed him off from everyday life. He did not choose the way of John the Baptist or the Essenes and retire to the desert to follow a religious vocation. His was a "public" ministry in which he was pressed and jostled by the crowds. He identified with the poor and outcast, assuming the burden of their cause. He made himself vulnerable to anyone in need, and defenseless before his enemies. That is the meaning of the cross.

From the human point of view, openness is probably the most difficult, if not impossible, demand made upon the community. The inherent tendency of human communities is to close themselves simply for self-preservation. Faced with an adversary, communities become self-defensive. But even apart from opposition they tend to become exclusive and concerned with their own life. Messianic openness means vulnerability and defenselessness, and can only be described with the paradox of losing one's life in order to save it. From the human side, such openness is one aspect of *metanoia,* described in Mark 8:34–35 as losing sight of self for the sake of the gospel. From the divine side, such community is possible only through the indwelling of the Spirit of God, the result of the miracle of rebirth.

Because of the way in which the mission of the church has been allied with western political expansion and military exploits, we need to be explicit on this point. The *messianic community is expendable,* and the posture of defenselessness, the cross, is an essential component of authentic witness. The church loses its authenticity if it seeks the protection of the secular authorities in alliances or cooperation with political and military powers. It loses its authenticity when, in a reflex of self-preservation, it becomes exclusive and separatist. It likewise loses its authenticity when, in the name of "service to the world," it allies itself with secular "liberation" movements that are essentially violent and self-defensive—the closed posture.

Dr. Vaughn Rees tells the beautiful story of such a modern-day miracle community in *The "Jesus Family" in Communist China.*[24] This band of several hundred Christians lived in total community prior to the Communist takeover. Guilelessly and defenselessly they dealt with envious neighbors, interpreting the teaching and example of Jesus quite literally. The final test came when the secular, violent Communists demanded their land in the name of all the people. They gladly gave not only their land, but as they moved to other less desirable territory they left the machinery which they had accumulated, because the people coming in would need it to keep up the production of the farm. They were expendable in the service of Christ for the world.

The open fellowship (*koinonia*) is a demonstrable witness, an expression of repentance and trust in the grace of God. Christian sharing is not simply an intra-group process. The New Testament word is to "do good *to all men*, especially the household of God" (Gal. 6:10). The community does not first nourish its own life to the point of abundance, and then share it in a ministry to those outside its membership. The first congregations of Macedonia set the example. "Their abundance of joy and their extreme poverty . . . overflowed in a wealth of liberality" (2 Cor. 8:2). *Koinonia* flows imperceptibly into *diakonia* (service), because what the open fellowship seeks for itself it seeks equally and simultaneously for the whole world.

A fourth authenticating characteristic of the Jesus community is *its broad concern with the whole of human life*. Its concern is for persons in their relation to God, themselves, and their fellows. No lesser scope is adequate to encompass its mandate.

The scope of Jesus' own ministry cannot be restricted to a single dimension of human need. Neither can it be compartmentalized into material, social, and spiritual, or into healing physical bodies and saving souls. His interest and care were always inclusive. Showing compassion for the poor, clothing the naked, healing the sick and blind, preaching the good news, accepting the outcasts, forgiving sins, feeding the hungry, casting out demons, restoring hope, teaching the preeminence of the spiritual—all were an integrated part of his ministry.[25]

We mentioned earlier the Church of the Savior's restructuring of the congregation for mission. The mission or spiritual ministries have been defined by the need which they see around them and the gifts which the Spirit of God has given to their group. Over the years they have been engaged in a broad spectrum of ministries such as spiritual retreats, housing developments for the poor, rescue and rehabilitation ministry centered in the Potter's House coffee shop, demonstrations for justice, preaching the gospel, Christian training classes, and intensive group discipline. The list could be continued. All of these ministries focused on the recovery of wholeness in Christ. Or, in other words, they were continuing the messianic mission of Jesus in seeking "the kingdom of God and his righteousness."

The objectives and goals of the messianic ministry, rather than its scope of activity, define its unique character and determine its strategy. In modern psychological terms Jesus was "inner-directed." He was not distracted by the urgent conflicting demands made upon him, but chose his own time and place for his service (Lu. 13:32). He moved in a framework of spiritual purpose. The whole of John's gospel makes this point with a luminous simplicity, focused explicitly in Jesus' act of washing his disciples' feet. "Jesus," wrote John, *"knowing that he had come from God and was going to God* . . . girded himself with a towel . . . and began to wash the disciples' feet"* (John 13:3–5). The scope of his concern was as broad as human need; the goal of his concern was the rule of God for the salvation of all mankind. And this continues to be the scope and goal of the messianic community.

The most explicit statement of the messianic commission is to "Go and make disciples of all nations, baptizing them . . . teaching them to live the way I have commanded you" (Matt. 28:19–20). The literal meaning of the New Testament word "disciple" is learner, but, as we noted, it implies more than a classroom pupil who comes for special religious instruction. In Jesus' day the learners became part of the teacher's household, and *followed* his way of life and teachings. They learned by being inducted into the household of the teacher and following a discipline. This clearly is the pattern envisioned in the great commission. To "baptize" is to induct into the life of the community as learner, and to "teach" what has been "commanded" is to communicate a way of life.

Far too long we have made unreal distinctions between the various areas of activity in the life and ministry of the church. The classical distinction was between the "religious" and the "secular" or "temporal." This translated into the "clerical" and "lay" vocations, and somehow in spite of all Protestant protestations, the clergy has always seemed more central and "churchly" than the laity. Indeed, the layperson's job has been seen as essentially outside the community. In more recent fundamentalist jargon, the distinction has been between the spiritual and social. In the past few years terms like "pre-evangelism," and "para-church" activities have begun to be used to designate priorities in the ministry of the church. Thus by implication the spiritual ministry of the community is defined by narrowing its concern to the individual's private religious faith.

The ministry of the community to human need is, indeed, essentially a spiritual one, if we mean by that *to bring the whole of human life under the control of the Spirit of God.* The "spiritual" is not a separate, non-physical segment of life which can be differentiated from bodily, material, psychological, and social aspects. And "spirituality" is not a superlative degree of piety or a particular species of being religious. Rather, it is participation in God's perspective and purpose for life. The spiritual is a quality of the whole person experienced as self-transcendence in openness to the Spirit of God, a dimension of reality and experience which both transcends and pervades the totality of authentic community.[26]

The mandate of Matthew 28:19, therefore, calls for more than evangelism, spiritual exercises, or liturgical and sacramental disciplines. It calls us to bring all of life under the discipline of Christ (intensive), and to spread his way of life throughout the nations (extensive). When thus understood, it becomes obvious that the commission implies and necessarily involves an authentic community of witness and concern for all facets of human life.

In summary, then, I have argued, in dialogue with various interpretative traditions, that the messianic community is itself the bearer of authentic witness. In living together as part of the "world" (the human social order), it anticipates and thus points to the plan and goal of God for human history. In Bonhoeffer's jargon I have maintained that the church not only requires *space in the world* to serve the worldly institutions in and under their own mandates, but a *worldly space* of its own. In more traditional Protestant terms I have attempted to show that the burden of authentic community witness rests, in the first instance, not on its preaching or in particular religious observances or "offices," but in the form and character of its life as a community of grace. Its witness of word and deed is an integrated whole for better or for worse.

Notes to Chapter VIII

1. M. M. Thomas, *Arunodayam* (published in India), May, 1971, p. 25, in an address given at the 50th anniversary of the founding of the Christian ashram movement in South India. The *Arunodayam* is the publication of Christavashram in Kottayam, Kerala.

2. Indeed, it is interesting to observe that the basic creation and cohesion of evangelicalism as a movement has been carried by the Billy Graham Evangelistic Association and cooperating agencies.

3. Dietrich Bonhoeffer, *The Cost of Discipleship*, Macmillan, 1959 (2nd ed.), p. 223. Cf. *Ethics*, Macmillan, 1965 (paperback), p. 201.

4. Bonhoeffer, *Ethics*, pp. 207f., 286ff. See note in his *Letters and Papers from Prison*, Macmillan, 1967 (rev. ed.), p. 104.

5. Bonhoeffer, *Cost*, pp. 226f.

6. *Ibid.*, p. 228.

7. Bonhoeffer, *Ethics*, pp. 300f.

8. Bonhoeffer, *Life Together*, S.C.M. Press, 1954, pp. 11, 15. Chapter 1, "Community," makes the point at considerable length.

9. Bonhoeffer, *Ethics*, p. 322.

10. *Ibid.*, pp. 300f.

11. *Ibid.*, p. 202: "The Church has neither the wish nor the obligation to extend her space to cover the space of the world."

12. Bonhoeffer, *The Way to Freedom*, Harper & Row, 1966, pp. 47f.

13. Bonhoeffer, *Letters*, p. 172.

14. *Bonhoeffer in a World Come of Age*, ed. by Peter Vorkink, II, Fortress Press, 1968, pp. 48f., 96f. Cf. "To be a Christian does not mean to be religious in a particular way, ... but to be a man—not a type of man but the man that Christ creates in us. It is not the religious act that makes the Christian, but participation in the sufferings of God." Bonhoeffer, *Letters*, p. 190.

15. Bonhoeffer, *Ethics*, p. 211: " ... the mandate of the Church impinges on all these mandates, for now it is the Christian who is at once labourer, partner in marriage, and subject of a government."

16. *Ibid.*, p. 201.

17. Bonhoeffer, *Letters*, p. 204.

18. Bonhoeffer, *Ethics*, p. 203.

19. He wrote in July 1944, "I discovered later [after writing *Cost of Discipleship*] and am still discovering right up to this moment that it is only by living completely in this world that one learns to have faith. . . . By this-worldliness I mean living unreservedly in life's duties, problems, successes and failures, experiences and perplexities." And Bethge wrote of him, "Bonhoeffer must have felt that the witness of *T.C.O.D.* had lost some of its concrete features of protest and attack." *Bonhoeffer*, p. 97.

20. See Harvey Cox, *The Secular City*, Macmillan, 1965; Richard P. McBrien, *The Church in the Thought of Bishop John Robinson*, Westminster, 1966; John A. T. Robinson, *The New Reformation*, Westminster, 1965; Gibson Winter, *The New Creation as Metropolis*, Macmillan, 1963. See also Chapter VI, "The Church as Servant," in Avery Dulles, *Models of the Church*, Doubleday, 1974, for a good critique.

21. Many biblical theologians have used the term "eschatological" to describe the church's relation to the final realization of God's rule. *Eschatos* is a New Testament word with special significance, meaning *end* or *finish*. Its synonym, *telos*, also means end in the sense of purpose or goal, without indicating that the end is also a finish or conclusion.

   The New Testament writers believed that God is moving the human drama toward a final climactic conclusion which is both fulfillment (*telos*) and finish (*eschatos*). History is not a movement in never-ending recurrent cycles. If it were, the ceaseless movement of history would be meaningless, and things that happen in history would have no "eschatological" significance, that is, no relation to a meaningful consummation. The Bible teaches that there is a climactic purposeful end.

Thus, in theological parlance the word *eschatos* or *eschaton* has come to be used as shorthand for all that is expected or hoped for in that consummation. And the term eschatological indicates a relationship to that end. Thus it describes the authentic community as the community which is a dynamic, anticipatory part of God's plan for bringing history to a successful conclusion in the final victory and rule of God in Christ.

22. This is the gist of Romans 8:18–30.

23. The kingdom of God, being the community's archetype, transcends every historical culture and every expression of it in the messianic community. It is supra-cultural. That is why the premillennialist tradition has always insisted that it is the cataclysmic work of God and placed it in the *eschaton*, that is, at the end of history.

24. Vaughn Rees, *The "Jesus Family" in Communist China*, Paternoster Press, 1959.

25. Perhaps Jesus' ministry to the demoniacs best epitomizes the integration of all these facets of work. All the dimensions of personal life—mind, body, soul, spirit, emotions—intersect in this ministry to those who had lost a sense of selfhood, and were beyond the inclusion and control of the social communities to which they belonged. Like our modern concept of psychosomatic relationships, the ancients' concept of spirits causing some physical and mental illnesses indicates their perception of the interrelated dimensions of human life, both personal and impersonal.

26. M. M. Thomas wrote that the spiritual being of man "does not at any time deny his involvement in the processes of animal nature and its necessities, . . . but gives a spiritual quality to it, for the involvement now takes place not within a structure of meaning and sacredness which the self in its freedom of self-transcendence chooses for itself. . . . Human spirituality, one might say, is the way in which man, in the freedom of his self-transcendence, seeks a structure of ultimate meaning and sacredness within which he can fulfil or realize himself in and through his involvement in the bodily, the material and the social realities and relations of his life on earth." *International Review of Missions* (April, 1973), p. 161.

INDEX

Adam, 81, 82, 105, 130
    as covenant creature, 82, 118
Agape, 70, 151
    Christian concept of, 134-37
    defined, 130, 132-34
Ames, William, 142
Anabaptism, 9, 138n
Apostle, as authentic witness, 19
Aristotle, 97, 98
    defines "human," 99, 105, 118
    defines virtue, 131
Ashrams, Christian, 168
Authentic
    meaning of, 13-16
    as original, 14
Authentic community. *See* Community, authentic
Authenticity, 38, 167
    and authority, 16
    and discipleship, 17
    and individuality, 15
    and orthodoxy, 10, 14
    popular meaning of, 19
    and sincerity, 14-15
Authentic selfhood, as gift of Holy Spirit, 89
Authentic witness
    beyond proclamation, 152
    and cross-cultural mission, 66
    defined, 10
    as life of church, 156
    role of individual in, 92-93

Authority and authenticity, 16

Barth, Karl
    church as "sign," 144-48
    influence of, 141, 175
    Social Gospel, rejection of, 176
Beaver, R. Pierce, 44, 46
Bible
    as collection of authentic documents, 56
    contextualizing process exemplified in, 53
    living, 61, 62-63
    nature of, as witness, 52-57
    translation of, 45, 62-64
Bonhoeffer, Dietrich, 119, 121, 180-81
    church "for the world," 148-49, 179
    church as "mandate," 177, 179
    church as sign, 148
    concept of church, 119, 176-80
    impact of, 175

Chalcedon, creed of, 29
Change, agents of, 47-48
Church, 35-36, 38
    as authentic community, 119, 120
    body of Christ, 22, 151
    Bonhoeffer's concept of, 176-80
    in continuity with Christ's witness, 20, 22

195

historical need for adaptation,
51-52
identity and role, 155-70
images of self-identity, 157-62
invisible, 141-44
as "mandate," 177, 179
mission of, 23, 174-75
as open community, 187
and salvation, 108
as sign of the Kingdom, 142-44,
149, 162-70
visible, form of, 178-80
in the world, 140-49, 161, 178
Church Growth movement, 116n,
143-44
Church of the Redeemer, 169
Church of the Savior, 169, 185, 189
City of man, 122-23, 124
Commission on World Mission and
Evangelism, 172-73
Communication
and community, 37-38
cross-cultural, 63-64
emphasis in witness, 59
Communism and communists, 94n,
101, 104. See also Socialism
Community
authentic, 90, 108, 109, 111-12,
118-20, 124, 128-29, 183
broken, 123
centrality of, 80
Christian, 121
and communication, 37-38
defined, 120-21
of discernment, 69-72
of discourse, 39
establishment of new, 21, 119
of interpretation, 71
messianic, 183-87, 190
old vs. new, 129-31
original, 123-24
of reconciliation, 40, 161
of repentance, 125
of salvation, 113
secular definition of, 76
self-identity in, 90-92
of shalom, 21, 81, 83, 122
of the Spirit, 23, 37, 93
spiritual ministry of, 191
of witness, 23
Contextualization, 51
criterion for, 61

defined, 58, 62
exemplified in New Testament,
53, 55
historical, 66
and indigenization, 57
problem of, 58-59
prophets as contextualizers, 53
Conversion, 106, 107
Corporate personality, 80, 94n
Covenant, 70, 82-85
Abrahamic, 90-91
messianic, 21, 86, 91
Mosaic, 90-91
Cross
authenticating sign, 21
symbol of vulnerability, 46
Culture
Christian, 67
non-Christian, 67, 174
relativity of, 59, 67, 68, 69
sacral, 68
secular, 68

Denck, Hans, 18
Denney, James, 30
Denominations, not equated with
"church," 35
Dialogue, principle of, 44-45
Disciple
concept of, 17, 25n, 190
defined, 18-19
Dispensationalism, 20, 143
Docetism, heresy of, 31-35
and mission strategy, 33

Emmanuel, 31
Enlightened self-interest, 103, 104
Eros, 130, 133-34
Evangelism, Protestant, 96, 103-12,
159, 166, 173
alliance with individualism, 103
mass evangelism, 111, 157-58
role of church in, 141, 159

Faculty psychology, 98
Forsyth, P. T., 16, 29, 166, 167
French Revolution, 100, 101
Fundamentalism, 166, 173

God
as self-communicating, 27-28
as self-disclosing, 70

Good news, 93. *See also* Gospel
Gospel, 20, 40, 60-61, 71
　personal, 109
　as self-communication of Christ,
　　38
　social, 105, 107, 109
　theology and, 60-61
　universal implications of, 54
Group solidarity, 79

Hendry, George, 30, 36-37
Hodge, Charles, 59
Holy Spirit
　agent of contextualization, 61
　agent of incarnation, 36
　ground-of-meeting, 37, 44
　and self-identity, 89
　true vicar of Christ, 22
Human family, goal of creation, 81
Human nature
　evangelical Protestant position
　　on, 107
　socialist-individualist debate con-
　　cerning, 102
Hutterites, 10, 138n, 160

Identification
　"insider" role, 41, 47
　meaning of, 41
　as mutuality, 43
　paternalism and, 43
　role relationships in, 47
　social analogue of incarnation,
　　40-41, 48
　and witness, 44
idios, 130, 131
"Image of God," 81, 82, 119, 132
　and concept of rational soul, 105
Incarnation, 27-38, 70
　defined, 29-30
　extension of, 35
　identification, social analogue of,
　　40-41, 48
　as self-communication of God, 28
"In Christ," 89, 130, 131
　as *agape*, 133-37
Individual
　alienation of, 78
　person distinguished from, 121
　role of, in witness, 92
　self-awareness of, 99, 100
　and society, 102

worth of, 77
Individual-in-community, 97, 112-13
　as corporate personality, 80
　Old Testament concept of, 79-80,
　　83
Individualism
　evangelical, 105, 106
　Greek precedents, 97, 98
　history of, 96-112
　and individuality, 84-85, 87
　rational, 104
　religious, 78, 96-98, 109-11
　and religious experience, 109-11
　and socialism, 100-04, 115n
Individuality, 83-85
　Jesus' concern with, 87-88
　in Psalms, 87
Interdependence, ideal of mutuality,
　44
International Congress on World
　Evangelism, 172

Jesus Christ
　authentic model, 16, 17
　as authentic man, 20, 119
　authentic witness, 67
　criterion for contextualizing, 61
　as "image of God," 18, 20
　imitation of, 18, 19
　individual identity of, 88
　and individuality, 87-88, 90
　as Lord, 17, 18
　as master, 17
　meaning of name, 28-29
　mission of, 20-23, 163-64, 186
　model of repentance, 125-26
　as rabbi, 17
　as savior, 28-29
　as second Adam, 89, 130
　as Son of God, 18
　as Spirit, 70, 91
　"Jesus community," 183, 189
Jesus Family," 188-89
Jordan, Clarence, 168, 169

Kāzantzakēs, Nikos, 30
Kenosis, 28
Kingdom of God, 20-21, 172,
　182-83, 186
　church as a sign of, 156, 162-70
　equated with church, 142-43
　See also Rule of God

Koinonia, 19, 21, 36, 61, 90, 130, 132, 134, 151, 189
Koinonia Farm, 168
Koinos, 130, 131-32
Kraemer, Hendrik, 37

Laissez faire, 101
Loewen, Jacob, 47
Logos (the Word), as self-expression of God, 27, 31
Lord's Supper, 151-52
Love. *See* Agape, Eros

Marx, Karl, and materialism, 96, 101, 103-04
Master, concept of, 17
Melanchthon, Philip, 142
Messianic commission, 190
Metanoia, 60, 130
    condition for community, 137, 151, 185
    defined, 124-28
    hallmark of authenticity, 167
Mission
    to "christianize" civilization, 174-75
    docetic strategy of, 33-34

Nativity, 28
Newbigin, Lesslie, 165
New Testament
    authentic unity of, 56
    authority of, 57
    exemplifies contextualization, 53, 55
    as original documents, 56
    plurality of perspectives in, 55
    witness character of, 57
Nicea, creed of, 29
Nida, Eugene, 45, 63

O'Connor, Elizabeth, 185
Octavianus, Petrus, 69
Orthodoxy
    and analysis of human nature, 98
    Protestant, 65-66, 97-98, 105, 124, 166
    theological origins of, 29

Paul
    as contextualizer, 54-55, 56
    and discipleship, 18

and identity "in Christ," 89-90, 97
Pentecost, 23, 39, 54, 89
Perkins, John, 162
Personalism, biblical, 96, 100, 112-13
Personhood
    biblical understanding of, 83, 112-13
    evangelical view of, 105-06, 108-09
    and I-Thou relationship, 121
Pre-theological stance, 64-65
Private property, 101, 103, 107
Prophets
    individuality in, 86-87
    self-consciousness of, 85-86
    solidarity of, with Israel, 86
    as spiritual contextualizers, 53
Protestantism. *See* Evangelicalism

Reconciliation, service of, 39-40
Reformation, as process of contextualization, 66
Religious experience, 109-11, 113
Repentance, 91, 93, 125. *See also* *Metanoia*
Riesi community, 156
Robinson, H. Wheeler, 80
Rule of God, 70. *See also* Kingdom of God
Rule of law, 107

Sacrament, 142
    authentic community as, 150-52
Salazar, Father Inocente, 44
Salvation
    biblical concept of, 112
    evangelical view of, 98, 106-08, 173-74
Satir, Virginia, 15
Schaff, Philip, 106
Self-awareness, growth of, 99-100
Self-communication, God's act of, 27, 38
Self-fulfillment, 15, 111, 133
Servant, stance of, 38-39, 46
Shalom, 21, 81, 122, 130
Sign
    Barth's concept of church as, 144-48

Bonhoeffer's concept of church as, 148
ecumenical concept of church as, 149-50
meaning of, 162-63
theological implications of, for church, 164-67
Sin, 39, 85, 132
nature and consequence, 122-23
Smith, Fred, 44-45
Snyder, Howard, 144
Social contract, 106
Social Gospel, 105, 107, 109, 174-76
Socialism
Communistic, 101, 104
and competition, 103
and individualism, 100-104, 115n
Society of Brothers, 160
Sojourners, 169
Soul
evangelical view of, 105-07
orthodox view of salvation, 98
rational, 105

Taylor, John V., 35-36, 37, 78

Theology
as contextual discipline, 66-67
definition of, 60, 64, 65
and gospel, 60-61
Translation, process of, 45, 63-64
Translations, vernacular, 62
Trilling, Lionel, 100
Truth, propositional, 61

Uppsala (1968), 166, 173

Verbal inspiration, importance of in orthodox theology, 148, 166
Vinay, Tullio, 156-57
Voice of Calvary, 162, 169
Vulnerability, 45-47, 188
cross as symbol of, 46
principle of, 45

Williams, Colin, 9, 177
Wilson, Monica, 99
Witness, cross-cultural, 60, 64, 65
Word, incarnate, 70-71
Wright, G. Ernest, 80, 84